The World of Animals

EAGLES

Editor : Winwood Reade

The World of Animals

EAGLES

LESLIE BROWN

Published simultaneously by

Arco Publishing Company, Inc.
219 PARK AVENUE SOUTH, NEW YORK, N.Y. 10003

and

Arthur Barker Limited
5 WINSLEY STREET, LONDON W1

Acknowledgements for Illustrations

The author and publishers are indebted to the following for permission to reproduce photographs in this book: Mr C. A. W. Guggisberg and Bruce Coleman Ltd for the photographs on pages 15 (*top*), 37, 87, 90 (*left*): Mr. E. Hosking for the photographs on pages 6, 15 (*bottom*), 16, 24, 26, 27, 30 and 31 (*bottom*) 35, 41, 47, 56, 59, 60, 71, 74 and 75 (*top*), 79, 90 (*right*), 93; Mr P. Jackson and Bruce Coleman Ltd for the photograph on page 20; Mr P. Johnson for the photographs on pages 23, 57, 64; Mr R. Kinne and Bruce Coleman Ltd for the photographs on pages 18, 34; Mr G. Maclean for the photograph on page 17; Mr N. Myers for the photographs on pages 9, 44; Mr C. E. Palmar for the photographs on pages 21, 30 and 31 (*top*), 49, 62, 67 (*bottom*), 78, 88, 94, and 95; Mr L. J. Parker for the photograph on page 54; Mr G. Pizzey and Bruce Coleman Ltd for the photographs on pages 11, 14, 25; Mr W. L. Puchalski and Bruce Coleman Ltd for the photograph on page 73; The Royal Society for the Protection of Birds for the photograph on page 91; Mr J. Savidge for the photograph on page 61; Mr W. R. Spofford for the photographs on pages 8, 51, 65; Mr P. Steyn for the photographs on pages 22, 28, 42 and 43, 89; and the Zoological Society of London for the photographs on pages 7, 10, 19, 53, 55.

Photographs on pages 12, 13, 33, 36, 38 and 39, 40, 46, 50, 58, 63, 67 (*top*), 68, 70, 72, 74 and 75 (*bottom*), 80, 81 (*top and bottom*), 82, 83, 84 and 85 and 86 were taken by the author.

Diagrams on pages 45, 47, 48, 52 are by Malcolm Ellis; on pages 91, 92 by Frank and John Craighead; and on pages 66, 69 (*top and bottom*) by the author.

Library of Congress Catalog Number 78-90242
Standard Book Number 668-01849-6
Printed in Great Britain
Bound in Holland

Contents

Acknowledgements   4

1   Define an eagle   7

2   Some facts about eagles   19

3   An eagle's day   35

4   Eagles as hunters   45

5   Eagles at home   63

6   The young eagle   79

7   Eagles and economics   89

CHAPTER ONE

Define an eagle

If the following question was posed in an examination paper it would not only puzzle the schoolboy or student for whom it was intended, but would tax the knowledge of many a serious ornithologist. What is an eagle? And what is not? And why? Probably the best definition of the term 'eagle' is that it is a large, powerful, rapacious diurnal bird of prey that is not a hawk, buzzard, vulture, falcon or kite – groups which include all the other diurnal raptors. Such a definition would fit well enough into the usage of the ancient Romans and Greeks, or even the Vikings. It would fit, for instance, the Greek root *etus*, meaning 'eagle', which today forms part of many of the generic names given to eagles. Aristotle, who made some of the earliest known observations on the territorial behaviour of eagles, also made a distinction between other large raptors and eagles. He would undoubtedly have accepted the above definition and it would fit well enough the Latin word *Aquila*, now applied to a genus, though even here we should run into difficulties. And it would also fit the Scandinavian word *örn*, pronounced 'erne' in English, and applied to one of two species of eagles that occur in Scandinavia. But once we leave Europe and venture into the tropics this simple definition of what is an eagle would break down.

Although many of the eagles are huge and powerful birds, much larger and more rapacious than any buzzard or kite, and larger than all but the largest vultures, some of their near relatives are quite small. Seen in isolation, these small eagles would be taken for hawks, and there is an overlap in their

Golden Eagle (*Aquila chrysaëtos*)
OPPOSITE: European Serpent Eagle (*Circaëtus gallicus*) – large yellow eyes and short toes that can grasp and immobilize a snake
OVERLEAF: *left* Golden Eagle (*Aquila chrysaëtos*) carrying ground squirrel (*Citellus paryii*)
right African Fish Eagle (*Haliaëtus vocifer*) – bare tarsi and sharp spicules on the soles of the feet to assist in holding slippery prey

OPPOSITE: Wedge-tailed Eagle (*Aquila audax*) – an Australian eagle that has to some extent adopted the scavenging role of vultures

Vulturine Fish Eagle (*Gypohierax angolensis*) lives largely on the fruits of oil palms and may be a convenient link between sea and fish eagles and the Old World vultures

predatory functions with buzzards, kites, and the larger goshawks, though not with the specialized falcons (except perhaps in South America, where there are many aberrant falcon types). For instance, Ayres' Hawk-eagle, of African tropical forests, is only a little larger than the European Goshawk, and like the Goshawk feeds on birds and squirrels caught in the treetops; it is much smaller than the larger buzzards and even smaller than some kites. Some of the Oriental Serpent Eagles of the genus *Spilornis* are smaller still. One of the smallest of all, the Nias Island Serpent Eagle, is a diminutive race of the widespread Crested Serpent Eagle, of which the largest continental forms are twice the size of the Nias Island bird and certainly big enough to have fitted Aristotle's definition of an eagle. If one were to see this little Snake Eagle perched on a tree, one would take it for a small hawk; but looking at it in the hand, its relation to larger birds would become clear.

We must therefore widen our rather nebulous definition of an eagle as a very large and predatory bird, not a buzzard, kite, hawk, falcon or vulture, to include the near relatives, even though they are much smaller, just as we include the Congo pigmies in the same species as Primo Carnera, the famous boxer. This is logical, but one feels that Aristotle, who thought of eagles as very large and rapacious birds, would at first have shaken his head in disgust.

Having accepted this as a working basis for saying what are eagles and what are not, we shall find, however, that some ornithologists, puzzled about the true relationships of some of the predatory birds they found in the tropics, have given way to meaningless compromises, and these we shall firmly reject. Thus we shall ignore the Australian Whistling Eagle (*Haliastur sphenurus*), which is nothing but a large kite; we shall also reject the insectivorous hawks of the genus *Butastur*, widespread in Asia and Africa and known in Africa – absurdly – as Grasshopper Buzzard Eagles. We shall also reject, with greater reluctance, the Grey Eagle-buzzard (*Geranoaetus melanoleucus*) of South American highlands, which is really only a big buzzard; but it so happens that in South America it is more difficult to draw a line between buzzard and eagle than elsewhere.

Rejecting these, there remain about fifty-nine of about 275 species of diurnal birds of prey, or almost a quarter, that can fairly be called eagles. They include members of twenty-

three genera, many of which are monotypic, that is to say, they contain only one species; examples are the Martial Eagle (*Polemaëtus bellicosus*) and Isidor's Eagle (*Oroaëtus isidori*). Some taxonomists would simplify this classification for example by submerging *Oroaëtus* in a larger genus *Spizaëtus*; but we need not concern ourselves with such subtleties of systematics.

In practice, the fifty-eight species can be conveniently divided into four main groups, as follows:

(1) The sea eagles and fish eagles, of the genera *Haliætus*, *Ichthyophaga* and *Gypohierax*. The largest members of this group

Ayres' Hawk-eagle (*Hieraaëtus ayresii*) – a small eagle with long legs that are probably an adaptation to bird-killing habits

are the huge Steller's and European Sea Eagles, and the smallest is the forest-loving Lesser Fishing Eagle (*Ichthyophaga nana*) of the far East. With these closely related birds we must, for want of a better place to put it, include the aberrant Vulturine Fish Eagle or Palm Nut Vulture, which lives largely on the fruits of oil palms, and which may be a convenient link between these sea and fish eagles and the Old World vultures. Sea eagles are actually more closely related to kites than they are to true eagles of the genus *Aquila*; they have bare tarsi (that is, their legs have no feathers below the knee or tarsal joint), and those that feed on fish have sharp spicules on the soles of their feet to assist in holding slippery prey.

(2) The serpent, snake, or harrier eagles, in which we include twelve species in five genera, *Circaëtus*, *Spilornis*, *Terathopius*, *Dryotriorchis* and *Eutriorchis*. Here we place the specialized Bateleur Eagle (*Terathopius ecaudatus*) (Nature's version of the flying wing), and the rare Congo and Madagascar Serpent Eagles (*Dryotriorchis spectabilis* and *Eutriorchis astur*). All of these feed essentially on snakes and other reptiles, though some, especially the Bateleur, also feed on carrion, or kill birds and mammals. Snake eagles are characterized by very large yellow eyes, which may perhaps indicate unusually keen vision, and short, rather thick strong toes which can immediately grasp and immobilize a snake. (One can see that if they had long thin toes a slim agile snake might slip through their grasp.) They are not immune to snake venom, but manage to avoid being bitten.

The largest of these birds is the Brown Snake Eagle (*Circaëtus cinereus*) of Africa, but nearly as large are the European Serpent Eagle (*Circaëtus gallicus*) and the continental races of the Crested Serpent Eagle (*Spilornis cheela*). As a group they are badly and confusingly named. They ought not to be called harrier eagles at all, though they are probably most closely related on one side to the harriers (genus *Circus*). They should be called snake eagles or serpent eagles on account of their main food, and such confusing names as 'Beautiful Wood Hawk' (for the Congo Serpent Eagle) should be discarded.

(3) A group of large eagles with bare tarsi, inhabiting South America, the Philippines and New Guinea. These include the solitary and crested eagles (*Harpyhaliaetus* and *Morphnus*) of South American forests; the Harpy Eagle (*Harpia harpyja*), the largest and most powerful of all the rap-

Brown Snake Eagle (*Circaëtus cinereus*) — upright stance and strong toes

Wedge-tailed Eagle (*Aquila audax*) – a species that has been badly persecuted on account of alleged killing of lambs

tors that feed on living prey; the scarcely smaller and nearly extinct Philippine Monkey-eating Eagle (*Pithecophaga jefferyi*); and a large eagle of New Guinea which for want of a better name is called the New Guinea Harpy Eagle (*Harpyopsis novae-guineae*). It is in this group that there is the greatest difficulty in separating buzzards from eagles, for in fact the latter are no more than overgrown, and in some cases very predatory and rapacious buzzards, with bare tarsi and other anatomical features that relate them to buzzards. What has happened, perhaps, is that some members of this group, living in areas where none of the larger sea eagles or true eagles occurred, took over the predatory functions of these birds and have not been supplanted. It is difficult to imagine any other bird of prey competing successfully now with the Harpy as a killer of monkeys, sloths and other mammals in Amazonian jungles, and there is no near competitor for the niche occupied by the Philippine Monkey-eater.

(4) The largest group, thirty species in nine genera, which we may call the true or booted eagles, with feathered tarsi; that is with feathers growing all over the leg down to the toes. This is not an adaptation to cold, for it occurs among tropical and arctic species alike. Among these Aristotle might feel at home, for they include nine members of the genus *Aquila* (one of which is as small as a buzzard) and the very large and powerful eagles of the genera *Stephanoaëtus*, *Polemaëtus* and *Oroaëtus*, which no one would think of as anything but eagles. The Indian Black Eagle, *Ictinaëtus*, is a curious bird, and is thought by some to be more closely related to kites than to eagles; but it looks like an eagle and Aristotle would probably have nodded his head in agreement. He would have been in more doubt about the 3 genera of hawk-eagles, *Hieraaëtus*, *Spizastur* and *Spizaëtus*, which live in woodland or forest, are very active predators, and are differentiated from *Aquila* and other large eagles not only on the basis of size, but also by the different proportions of wings and tail. Forest life, as we shall see, demands a different shape and different hunting methods to life in open terrain, and these forest hawk-eagles usually have rather long tails and short rounded wings. Some of them, as already mentioned, are so small that they behave much like the larger sparrowhawks.

All these true or booted eagles are more or less active predators, some of them among the swiftest and most vigorous of all birds of prey. Some members of the genus *Aquila* live on comparatively inactive creatures like frogs, and several regularly eat carrion. The Australian Wedge-tailed Eagle (*A. audax*), in a continent where there are no vultures, has to an extent taken over the latter's scavenging function. The very striking black Long-crested Eagle (*Lophaëtus occipitalis*) of Africa behaves like a buzzard, killing nothing large and subsisting mainly on mice and rats. As already mentioned, there is an overlap in predatory function between the smaller eagles and other groups of diurnal raptors.

Thus we have our fifty-nine eagle species more or less classified and defined, albeit in rather arbitrary groupings of more or less close relatives which are, in turn, not closely related to other groups of eagles. It will be evident that it is much more difficult to simplify the classification of eagles than it is, for instance, to do so for penguins or pelicans. Eagles perform a great variety of predatory functions, and one is even a vegetarian. They vary in size from very large to moderately large, and they inhabit most areas of the globe from arctic wastes to tropical forests, snowy mountains and stark deserts. They eat anything, dead or alive, from termites to dead elephants and whales. Yet, varied though they are, a common thread runs through their lives, setting them in some minor ways apart from other diurnal birds of prey. Aristotle would have argued about it a good deal, as any good scientist should, but in time he would have come to recognize that there is a certain logic in calling all these birds 'eagles' and not lumping them under the much more ambiguous word 'hawk'.

ABOVE: Martial Eagle (*Polemaëtus bellicosus*) – a large and powerful eagle
RIGHT: Long-crested Eagle (*Lophaëtus occipitalis*) – behaves like a buzzard and subsists mainly on mice and rats

ABOVE: Martial Eagle (*Polemaëtus bellicosus*)
OPPOSITE: Philippine Monkey-eating Eagle (*Pithecophaga jefferyi*)

CHAPTER TWO

Some facts about eagles

The type of information that most people seem to want about eagles concerns their size (especially their wingspan which has not often been accurately measured), their strength (which includes details of the size of prey they are capable of killing), and sometimes the age to which they can live. Few people realize that there are any but very large eagles, or any that live essentially on small, weak, easily caught creatures. They are almost universally thought of as birds of legendary size and power, and the idea that they are able to kill and carry off babies is often still prevalent.

Although some eagles are very large, and though they are, for their size, the most powerful birds in the world, their actual dimesions are very often exaggerated. The largest eagle in the world is the South American Harpy Eagle. A Harpy was a mythical wreaker of vegeance, and certainly the Harpy Eagle, with its flaring double crest and huge hooked beak, looks vengeful enough. The female Harpy, which is both much larger and more powerful than the male, weighs at least fifteen or twenty pounds, and has a tarsus (the lower part of the leg) as thick as a child's wrist, ending in a foot spanning nine inches and equipped with huge talons more than an inch and a half long. Such a foot could obviously drive the talons right through a young monkey and kill it almost instantly.

The sheer size and weight of the female Harpy Eagle might result in aerodynamic problems in the forest environment in which she lives. Harpies have not been seen soaring like other eagles, and it is possible they do not because of their weight.

Philippine Monkey-eating Eagle (*Pithecophaga jefferyi*) – in danger of becoming extinct

OPPOSITE: Golden Eagle (*Aquila chrysaëtos*) – trained by falconers in Siberia to fly at wolves

However, it would be unwise to dogmatize about a species that is rather little known, for in the African Crowned Eagle (*Stephanoaëtus coronatus*), also a forest dweller with much the same general form, both sexes soar high with ease, even when fully fed or carrying prey. The male Harpy is very little heavier than the male Crowned Eagle (nine to ten pounds as compared with eight to nine) and not as heavy as a female. Again basing the comparison on the Crowned Eagle's dimensions, a female Harpy might span about seven and a half feet, and a male more than six feet. However, Harpies and other large eagles that live in forests have rather short, broad wings relative to their height, so the fact that the world's largest eagle spans less than eight feet does not necessarily mean that there are no eagles spanning more than eight feet. If the female Harpy had the same proportions as a Golden Eagle (*Aquila chrysaëtos*) – a long-winged species living in open country – she would span over nine feet.

Harpies are extremely powerful birds, capable of killing

African Crowned Eagle (*Stephanoaëtus coronatus*) – the wingspan of one of the large forest dwelling eagles; although heavily built it will soar

OPPOSITE: Steppe Eagle (*Aquila nipalensis*) – Eurasian race of Tawny Eagle

OPPOSITE: Verreaux's Eagle (*Aquila verreauxii*) at nest; typical cliff site

ABOVE: Immature African Hawk-eagle (*Hieraaëtus fasciatus spilogaster*)

White-bellied Sea Eagle (*Haliaëtus leucogaster*)
note length of wing in proportion to tail

monkeys, sloths, and probably small deer in the American forests. Though too little is known about them to state with certainty the largest size of animal they could kill, they are undoubtedly formidable. A falconer who kept a female found that she was readily manned to come to the fist. The problem was not to get her to come, but rather to be sufficiently padded, braced, and protected to withstand the impact of her arrival. Again, the African Crowned Eagle is known on occasion to kill antelopes of more than thirty pounds weight, so that a female Harpy could probably kill an animal weighing fifty pounds. However, she certainly could not lift such prey, and perhaps could not lift animals that a Crowned Eagle could lift, because of the problems posed by her own great weight.

We may, in fact, suggest that a Harpy is about as large as an eagle can be and still fly well enough to hunt at all. Those who have watched them say that they are dexterous in flight among the treetops, as is the African Crowned Eagle. Someone should watch Harpies at the beginning of the breeding season to see if they have an aerial display which involves high soaring, as do most other forest eagles.

Another forest-loving eagle, very nearly as large as the Harpy, is the Philippine Monkey-eating Eagle. The only weight I have is for a male weighing just over ten pounds (4,650 grams), whereas four male Harpies weighed nine to ten pounds (4,000–4,600 grams). These figures do no more than indicate that the Monkey-eater is only slightly smaller than the Harpy, though one has the impression, from individuals in zoos, that it is a slighter, lighter bird in relation to its wingspan, with less powerful but still very formidable feet.

Unfortunately, the impressive size of the Monkey-eater in the Philippines, and the fact that it is a favourite in zoos, has almost led to its extinction through trophy hunting and capture for sale. There are probably less than a hundred left in the wild state, and this may be the world's rarest eagle. The Harpy, with a very much more extensive range, is still relatively common. More exact data about these great birds is lacking because no very detailed field study has been made of either.

Next on the list in sheer size is Steller's Sea Eagle (*Haliaëtus pelagicus*), a magnificent black and white bird with a huge arched yellow bill, perhaps the most impressive looking of all birds of prey. It inhabits Kamschatka and neighbouring coast lines, and the larger rivers of northeast Siberia. It too is huge, females weighing from fifteen to twenty pounds (6,800–8,970 grams) and males eleven to thirteen pounds (5,000–7,000 grams), according to Russian figures. I have not seen a span measurement, but by comparison with its close relative the European Sea Eagle or Erne, a female would span up to 7½ ft, or perhaps 8 ft. The wings of sea eagles, of the genus *Haliæetus*, are longer in proportion, and the tails shorter than are those of the very large forest-loving eagles, though still not relatively as long as those of eagles that live in mountainous or open country. Steller's Sea Eagle feeds mainly on fish,

Wedge-tailed Eagle (*Aquila audax*) – an individual with a wingspan of eight ft three ins has been reported

especially perhaps Pacific salmon; but they are known to kill birds as large as a Capercaillie (*Tetrao urogallus*) and mammals as large as a seal calf, perhaps 10–15 lbs in weight. But in relation to their size sea eagles are not usually such potent predators as are some of the smaller eagles.

The European Sea Eagle is only a little smaller than Steller's and fractionally less impressive. It is the fourth largest eagle in the world, and the first of those mentioned for which there is a fairly good series of measurements, covering a number of individuals, on which to base maxima and averages. Females weigh 8–14½ lbs (3,650–6,560 grams); they span 6 ft 7 ins– 7 ft 9 ins (2,020–2390 mm); there are probably individuals with a wingspan of 8 ft. Males are smaller weighing 6½–11 lbs (3,075–4,985 grams) and spanning 6 ft 3 ins to 7 ft 4 ins (1992–2250 mm); they are relatively longer winged in rela- tion to their weight than are the females. Like their congeners they live mainly on fish; but they take a fair number of birds and such animals as young seals, hares and deer calves. It is rather unlikely that they kill anything heavier than 20 lbs.

Next in order of size, and the largest eagles living in open country, would be the Martial Eagle of Africa (*Polemaetus bellicosus*) and the largest race of the Holarctic Golden Eagle, the Russian and Siberian (*Aquila chrysaëtos daphanea*), locally known as the Berkut. There are not many reliable details on wingspan, weight, etc. for either of these species, but Martial Eagles would probably span about 6½–8 ft, and females weigh about 13–14 lbs (5,900–6,200 grams). The recorded weights for Siberian Golden Eagles are much less, but may not have been from fully healthy birds. On the basis of wing measure- ment, the largest Siberian Golden Eagles would span just under 8 ft (2,310 mm), and Martial Eagles would be slightly smaller. The point could be settled by measuring any available females in zoos, or in the hands of falconers, or those that happen to be shot by any collectors. Why this measurement is so seldom recorded by collectors is a mystery.

The best series of measurements available for any large eagle are for the Australian Wedge-tailed Eagle. Since large numbers of this eagle are killed annually because of their supposed depredations on lambs, more dead specimens have been available to measure. In one series of forty-three birds spans varied from 6 ft 3 ins to 7 ft 3 ins (1,905–2,200 mm), and weights from 5½–10 lbs (2,495–4,346 grams). An indivi-

Crested Serpent Eagle (*Spilornis cheela*) – feeds on snakes and other reptiles

dual with a wingspan of 8 ft 3 ins (2,538 mm) was recorded, and still larger birds reported. Until, however, some naturalist has actually measured and recorded such eagles of more than 9 ft or 10 ft wingspan, I prefer to stick to the facts as known and to say that the largest living eagles weigh around 20 lbs, and span less than eight and a half feet. A good cure for flights of fancy is to draw the birds with chalk on a wall, and see what one with a wingspan of 11 ft would look like. Any other eagle in the world is smaller in some dimension than those already mentioned.

The largest eagles are not necessarily the most powerful, though there seems no other natural advantage in sheer size but greater power. The African Crowned Eagle whose habits are, through my own studies, perhaps better known than those of any other eagle in the world, is certainly rather smaller than the Martial Eagle, with shorter, broader wings, and usually weighs no more than $8\frac{1}{2}$ lbs (4,000 grams). I have handled a male weighing 9 lbs (4,100 grams approximately) who, although a large male, was not the largest I have seen and was mated to a female larger and heavier than himself. This particular male had a wingspan of just over six feet (1,850 mm). He was thus considerably smaller than several of the eagles we have mentioned so far.

However, a few days before I handled this dead male, I knew that either he or his rather larger spouse killed a young bushbuck weighing 30–35 lbs. I have never known any kill of this size made by a Martial Eagle, and it is the largest animal I have personally known any species of eagle to kill. Golden Eagles, in particular, are occasionally reported to kill such animals as pronghorn antelope or deer, perhaps heavier than this bushbuck, but only in hard winter conditions when the eagles would be very hungry and the animals disabled or at a disadvantage in heavy snow. Siberian Golden Eagles are trained by falconers to fly at wolves, which might weigh 100 lbs; but it is the falconer who kills the wolf, the eagle only holds it. In the case of the bushbuck the animal was young, but otherwise perfectly healthy and not at a disadvantage. Another pair of Crowned Eagles not far away were said to have killed a prize Burmese tomcat weighing 17 lbs, who was himself so savage that he was not allowed to play with the family and was kept in a special enclosure.

These are more formidable or heavier animals than I have

Tawny Eagle (*Aquila rapax*) – the commonest eagle in the world

Bateleur Eagle (*Terathopius ecaudatus*) – a wingspan of about five and a half to six ft

ever known a Martial Eagle to tackle; yet the male Crowned Eagle, bringing a portion of the bushbuck weighing 2½ lbs to the nest, had great difficulty in flying and most of the bushbuck was eaten either by a leopard or a hyena, as the eagles could not carry it away all at once.

It will be quite evident that if a large eagle can kill an active strong young bushbuck, weighing 30 lbs, it could theoretically kill a 10 lb baby, or even a toddler. But an eagle cannot lift such weights and large animals must be dismembered, removed piecemeal, and perhaps cached in trees until needed. The taking of babies may be an ancestral primate human memory and fear, but has not been credibly reported in recent times and can safely be ignored.

These facts, then, relate to the upper end of the eagle scale of size, weight, wingspan and killing ability. At the other end of the scale is the diminutive Nias Island Serpent Eagle (*Spilornis cheela asturinus*), meaning 'like a hawk', which would span only a little over 3 ft. However, it has not to my knowledge been weighed and measured, so it is pointless to guess at its dimensions. Better known, and among the smallest of eagles, are the European Booted Eagle (*Hieraaëtus pennatus*) and the African Ayres' Hawk-eagle (*Hieraaëtus ayresii*). A male Booted Eagle weighed about 1 lb 5 oz (595 grams) and two spanned 3 ft 10 ins and 3 ft 11 ins (1,162 and 1,210 mm). The New Guinea race of a related species, the Little Eagle (*Hieraaëtus morphnoïdes*) may be still smaller, for a young bird weighed only about 1 lb (483 grams), and the wing measurement is less than that of a Booted Eagle. Ayres' Eagles, on available weights, are larger, a male weighing 714 grams and two females 879 and 940, or about 1½–2 lbs, for the species as a whole.

These are about the smallest existing eagles. The Nias Island Serpent Eagle presumably lives on small snakes, while the Ayres' and Booted Eagles kill birds, and an occasional forest mammal. Ayres', which is a species I have studied intimately, feeds mainly on small birds of the treetops, which it catches with breathtaking speed and agility. I have personally seen a Booted Eagle in Spain stoop at a Red-legged partridge, and the largest bird we have ever known the Ayres' to kill was a guineafowl, perhaps a young one, but weighing at least two pounds, or rather more than the Ayres' Eagle itself.

Between these extremes there is a whole range of eagles of

different sizes and proportions, living on a great variety of prey, including small mammals, birds, snakes, frogs, and carrion. Some of them are rather generalized sorts of birds; others are very highly specialized. A few go in for piracy, taking prey from others often larger than themselves, a habit often associated with carrion feeding. Some are quite inoffensive and weak, others fierce and, for their size, the most powerful of avian predators. All these variations cannot be discussed, but it may be worthwhile to mention a few general features and some of the more extreme examples of specialization.

If I were asked what is the most common species of eagle in the world, I should unhesitatingly plump for the Tawny Eagle (*Aquila rapax*) which, with its Eurasian races formerly called Steppe Eagles (*A. nipalensis*), inhabits a huge tract of open arid and semi-arid country from easter Europe to western China, south through India and Africa to the Cape of Good Hope. This species is certainly the most widespread of all in open country in Africa. It would be pointless to suggest any possible world population without evidence, but I would think that it is the one species that perhaps numbers more than 200,000. It is also rather a good example of the advantages of non-specialization.

Tawny Eagles are considerably smaller than Golden Eagles but otherwise rather like them, dull dark or pale brown in colour, with rather long wings relative to their weight. The various races weigh from 3–10 lbs (1,540 to 4,850 grams), the largest females of the Eastern Steppe Eagle being as big as Golden Eagles; most weigh less than $5\frac{1}{2}$ lbs (2,500 grams), smaller than the smallest Golden Eagle. Tawny Eagles usually eat such small mammals as the rodents that swarm on Siberian steppes, or the mole rats of the Ethiopian and East African plains. But they will turn their hand to anything from a termite to a hare, go in for piracy, scavenge for scraps, or eat carrion. I have seen Tawny Eagles clustered round the mouth of a termite burrow as the winged insects swarmed out after rain to begin their nuptial flight. I have watched them pursue and take prey from divers other raptors, larger or smaller than themselves. I have known them to come to the sound of gunshots, evidently in anticipation of obtaining a wounded bird, at a watering-place frequented by sand-grouse. In North Africa and India they commonly go for carrion, and scavenge round camp sites and villages, though this habit is less prevalent in southern Africa. They breed on the ground in eastern Europe (Steppe Eagles), in trees in Africa and India, and on cliffs on mountains of eastern Asia. Some individuals kill many birds, and one pair that lives near a flamingo flight-line in the Kenya Rift Valley catches them in flight with a swift stoop; they have also been known to take such animals as hares and the Bat-eared fox (*Octocyon megalotis*). A very versatile bird, in fact, so much so that it has been able to occupy a large part of the earth's surface and has become numerically the dominant eagle on it.

Intense specialization is less likely to be beneficial than versatility, except locally where a particular set of circumstances warrants it, but on occasion it, too, pays. The Bateleur Eagle of Africa is a very specialized bird, with very long wings in relation to its bodyweight, scarcely any tail, and the habit of flying for many hours a day about fifty to two hundred feet above the ground at an airspeed of thirty-five to fifty miles an hour. This species is also unusual among eagles in that it is sexually dimorphic, males being instantly recognizable from females at up to a mile away. On the basis of voice, breeding habits, structure of the feet, and other features, the nearest relatives are to be found among the Snake Eagles.

Bateleurs weigh $4\frac{1}{2}$–$6\frac{1}{2}$ lbs (1,927–2,950 grams), females being the heavier. They span about $5\frac{1}{2}$–6 ft (1,727–72 mm) in those measured; and although they appear to have very long wings in relation to their size, in fact their wing length in relation to bodyweight is considerably less than that of similar sized Tawny Eagles that live in the same sort of country. Bateleurs' wings are also rather narrow, so that their wing-loading is decidedly higher than that of other eagles of about the same weight. This in itself is perhaps a specialization for high-speed gliding over great distances. Bateleurs, by means of their unique body and wing structure, are able to glide apparently without effort, for many hours daily, travelling perhaps 200–300 miles every day. In this way they cover a vast area of ground, which they scan from a moderate height, descending to kill small mammals, snakes, and some ground birds; to feed on carrion, or to chase a vulture in piracy similar to that used by the Tawny Eagle. They are structurally specialized, but in their range of feeding habits and prey they are almost as versatile as Tawny Eagles.

Bateleurs are able to fly far and fast during the day. The

slowest flier among eagles is probably the Indian Black Eagle, which has very long, broad, soft and flexible primaries, unlike the stiff feathers possessed by most eagles. The Indian Black Eagle feeds upon small helpless creatures, such as nestlings in their nests, or even eggs. To find such prey it may be an advantage to be able to fly very slowly over forests or hillsides, while the Bateleur may find it an advantage to travel fast.

As a rule eagles do not appear to be very fast fliers, though, because of their size, this is often an optical illusion. I have watched a Martial Eagle, gliding in almost level flight, easily outpace a male Peregrine Falcon that stooped at it from behind. Peregrine Falcons in full stoop are credited with being able to travel at well over 100, perhaps even more than 200, miles an hour. This particular Peregrine was not stooping very fast, but the eagle, by slightly altering the angle of glide, was able to accelerate probably to more than 100 mph., and easily escape the falcon. A Golden Eagle in Scotland has been timed to travel at 120 mph over a considerable distance; and it is very likely that they too can on occasion approach 200 mph. Certainly I have seen Golden Eagles stooping at speeds apparently no less than those attained by Peregrine Falcons, though eagles do not usually stoop at such speeds in order to kill their prey.

The age to which eagles may live is another subject of perennial interest. In estimating it we must make the distinction betweeen the potential age, which is the maximum age to which an eagle might live, and the age to which such birds actually do live on the wild state. The potential age has been quite often reached in zoos, where there are records of large eagles that have lived for more than forty years. Golden Eagles in zoos have lived for forty-one to forty-eight years, but an Imperial Eagle (*Aquila heliaca*) reputed to be fifty-six years old, is more doubtful. There was a Bateleur of forty-four years of age in the London Zoo until recently, and I have been able to find another authentic record of a Bateleur, fifty-five years

ABOVE: Golden Eagle (*Aquila chrysaëtos*) – capable of flying 120–200 mph and of stooping at a speed comparable to the Peregrine Falcon (*Falco peregrinus*)
BELOW: Imperial Eagle (*Aquila heliaca*) – a large eagle that in captivity may live to forty years old or more

old and still alive. However, records of anything over fifty years old are in general very doubtful; and even anything of over forty years of age must be scrutinized rather carefully.

While any large eagle should be able to live to around forty, it is most unlikely that even large eagles ever approach such an age in the wild state. It is quite possible to calculate theoretically the age to which eagles should live as, in a stable population, it is only necessary for a pair to rear enough other adults to replace themselves in their lifetime. Undisturbed eagle populations appear very stable indeed – the same nests and territories are occupied year in and year out for generations. Thus we may assume that in the wild state eagles need not, and on the average probably do not, live longer than is necessary to replace themselves.

This question is discussed more fully in Chapter 6. Here we need only say that large eagles such as Golden Eagles, rearing about four young in five years per pair, need only live about ten years in the wild state to replace themselves with sexually mature successors, assuming that three-quarters of the young die before sexual maturity. As a general rule it is not necessary for wild eagles to live much longer than this, though there may be exceptions in areas where some species appear to have very low breeding success, and must consequently live longer in order to rear their own replacements.

In the wild state the age of eagles is difficult to ascertain, but it can be done if one watches the same nest long enough. At one nest of a pair of Crowned Eagles that I have watched for nineteen years the second female incumbent arrived in 1952, bred that year and on four other occasions, and disappeared in 1961. She was then in her ninth adult year and since such eagles probably do not attain sexual maturity until they are four or five years old, she cannot have been less than thirteen, and may have been fifteen or sixteen when she disappeared. We assume she must have died (though there is no proof) for such large eagles certainly remain paired as long as any one of the pair is alive. When one dies or disappears, however, the survivor does not – as is sometimes stated – pine, but at once obtains another mate if one is available.

By studying the number of changes of mates over a period of years, one may arrive at very similar conclusions as to the average age of the eagles in the wild state. In the Crowned Eagle, which is probably better known in this respect than any other, there is a change of mate every six to seven years at nests I have studied, which corresponds well with other data. Wild Crowned Eagles, and probably other large eagles of similar size, may live ten to twelve years as adults or fourteen to sixteen years altogether. The oldest birds, in the wild state, known to me at present are a female which is at least eleven as an adult, and a male of the same age; both are, accordingly, at least fifteen, probably sixteen or seventeen. The male is probably the younger of the two, for he first appeared after the disappearance of another male, whereas the female was at the nest site when I first found it and has been there ever since.

The size of the eagle affects the age to which it lives. In Africa, for instance, smaller eagles breed rather more often, and rear more young than do the larger eagles. Thus, if one assumes that the age of the birds must be related to the number of young reared, the smaller eagles do not need to live so long. However, again the records are very scanty. One Ayres' Eagle known to me, living on the same hill as the fifteen-year-old male Crowned Eagle, is also about the same age, or a year or so younger, as he too appeared in 1958. He has had four mates and one is still alive; on this basis we can assume that the average age of Ayres' Eagle is less than in the Crowned Eagle.

Eagles are very often the subject of much conjecture, fancy, or exaggeration. The best answer to wild tales of their size, ferocity, and legendary ability to live to great age is in painfully acquired statistics and records. Such data cannot be quickly obtained, but every collector or falconer could easily add interesting facts to our knowledge of eagles if he would only record the weights, wingspan, and wing area of the birds he shoots or possesses. And the very rare field observers who have enough time or inclination to watch at eagles' nests for many years could not do better than add to our knowledge of subjects such as the age to which individual eagles live, either by direct observation, or by recording the changes of mates at a number of sites, accumulating data on the frequency of such changes, and through this, the average age of the adult wild eagles.

Crowned Eagle (*Stephanoaëtus coronatus*) – this particular female has been watched by the author since 1959; she is at least fifteen years old and still going strong

CHAPTER THREE

An eagle's day

It is no easy matter to ascertain what any bird does all day long, much less an eagle, which can fly at 100 mph in any direction it likes, perhaps covering rough mountainous terrain that an observer can only cover slowly on foot. Thus most accounts of the diurnal activity of eagles necessarily suffer from the disadvantage that they are pieced together from scrappy observations made at different times of day, while the exact details of any individual bird's behaviour are very difficult to record. Attempts have been made to ascertain an eagle's actions by means of small radio transmitters; but apart from the difficulty of picking up the signals from distances of more than two miles, some of the eagles themselves did not remain long in the area and the result was only of limited success.

However, long observation of many species in the field provides a fair basis for a composite picture of an eagle's day. The details vary a good deal according to various factors, such as the weather, the time of year, whether or not the eagle itself is hungry and feels obliged to hunt, and the size of the prey habitually taken. Some eagles are relatively much more active than others, ranging over wide areas; while some, for instance the African Fish Eagle (*Haliaëtus vocifer*) will often remain the whole day in a comparatively small area. Despite these qualifications one may attempt a general account of the behaviour of a particular species, and relate it to that of others.

The best-known eagles in the world are probably the Golden Eagle of Europe and America and the African Crowned Eagle.

African Fish Eagle (*Haliaëtus vocifer*) – a species that will often remain in a comparatively small area for the whole day

OPPOSITE: Bald Eagle (*Haliaëtus leucocephalus*) – observations on this species suggest that, having fed soon after dawn, these eagles are comparatively inactive during the rest of the day when the weather is cold and dull

Roost and nest site of Verreaux's Eagle (*Aquila verreauxi*) on hyrax infested cliff

But in the first case the mountainous terrain, in which the eagles range over extensive territories covering ten to sixty square miles, makes direct observation difficult. Rather intensive work is at present being carried out on the behaviour of the Golden Eagle in Montana; but the results that I have seen do not include any account of diurnal activities. In the Golden Eagle, moreover, the situation would be complicated by the difficulty of recognizing one individual from another at a distance, often in poor light and cloudy weather – as in the Scottish Highlands, where adjacent pairs commonly hunt over 'communal' areas at the borders of their territory. In the Crowned Eagle, although behaviour at the nest has been very intensively studied, the forest habitat of this species makes locating individuals away from the nest extremely difficult. So neither of these two well-known species are very suitable for our purpose.

Verreaux's Eagle (*Aquila verreauxii*), a near relative of the Golden Eagle, inhabiting rocky hills in Africa, would be a good species for our purpose. Being coal-black with a white back, it cannot possibly be mistaken for any other species. Moreover, the hills on which it lives are often isolated by many miles from other hills on which other pairs may live, so that confusion with other neighbouring pairs is minimized. It is often possible, by watching from the top of such a hill, to keep the eagles in view for long periods. Though no one to my knowledge has ever watched a pair of Verreaux's Eagles throughout the day to see what they did, a good composite picture can be obtained from these birds.

Apart from the nest during the breeding season, the easiest place at which to locate an eagle is on the roost in the early morning. Observation of roosting Verreaux's Eagles shows that they are very often on the wing shortly after dawn. At first light they preen, and perhaps bask in the rays of the rising sun, if the cliff on which they roost is not shaded. Then they take wing, but not necessarily to hunt. They may simply glide to and fro over the rock face for a period, then perch on a ledge or on a tree at the top of the cliff. This behaviour naturally varies according to whether they are hungry or not; if they are hungry they will probably hunt in earnest. On a wet morning, hungry or not, they will remain on their roost ledges until very much later, drying their feathers and preening. They may be forced to stay there for two or three hours after

Rock hyrax (*Procavia and Heterohyrax spp.*) – typical prey of Verreaux's Eagle

first light, for their plumage is not efficient when wet, and they are reluctant to fly. With the exception of such species as the Scottish Golden Eagle, which lives in a perennially wet climate, a wet morning seems to delay hunting and flight in all eagles I have observed.

The rock hyrax (*Procavia* and *Heterohyrax spp.*) on which Verreaux's Eagles feed are almost exclusively diurnal, though one may hear them calling at night. They usually feed in groups, starting two to three hours after sunrise, continuing until about eleven A.M. They return to their holes during the hottest hours of the day, and feed again in the afternoon, from about three o'clock to sunset, with a peak during the last hour of daylight. Hyrax also spend much of their time out in the open, playing or basking on rocks in the early morning, still more between nine o'clock and noon, reducing this activity in the heat of the afternoon, but basking again towards sunset. The eagles have the best chance of catching their prey when feeding some distance from their holes, or when basking on rocks in the early morning and late afternoon. The early morning departure from the roost and flying about may be real hunting, in an attempt to catch a basking hyrax, but just as often it is in the nature of exercise.

When hunting in earnest Verreaux's Eagles fly low over cliffs and hillsides dotted with boulders. The pair are often in sight of one another, and are most likely to kill their prey during the morning, but if they fail they may hunt again in the evening. In the tropics, where the length of the day is about twelve hours, they usually kill during the morning, on the evidence of times at which kills are brought to the nest; this is not an entirely reliable guide, but gives a fair indication.

Once they have killed, the eagles will usually feed on the prey together; either sex will feed on a kill made by the other, though the bird which makes the kill will satisfy his or her appetite first. This, and the habit of hunting fairly close together, also applies to several other eagles, for instance the African Hawk Eagle (*Hieraaëtus fasciatus spilogaster*), and is probably one way by which the pair-bond – which lasts as long as any member of the pair is alive – is maintained outside the breeding season. When a pair is feeding together it is possible to ascertain which bird made the kill and fed first by observing the state of the crop. A fully fed eagle has a crop which projects as a sizeable lump on its upper breast. It is

Verreaux's Eagle (*Aquila verreauxi*) at nest; tree site is unusual

likewise possible to ascertain whether an eagle which is apparently hunting is hungry or not; if it has a full crop it is not hungry, and is probably not therefore actually hunting.

The Verreaux's Eagles may not be hungry, in which case they are unlikely to hunt seriously at all, but will content themselves with flying about, and perching for long hours on ledges or on trees on the cliffs in their territory. It is not necessary for large eagles that live on prey large enough to provide more than one meal to kill every day, and they do not. Long observation of the Crowned Eagles at my house leads me to conclude that, except when they have small young in the nest, they kill on an average of once every three or four days. A large kill may last them much longer than this. A pair of Verreaux's Eagles, with a food requirement of about half a pound (200 grams) per adult per day, feeding mainly on hyrax weighing from two to seven pounds, could live on a small one for two days and on a large one for a week. They would eat more than their daily ration at one sitting; but once gorged, would not feel hungry or desire to kill again for several days.

This sort of consideration does not apply to all eagles; for instance, small eagles such as Wahlberg's (*Aquila wahlbergi*) – living on lizards, small mammals and some gamebirds – or Ayres' Hawk-eagle – living mainly on small woodland and forest birds – probably have to kill every day, perhaps even more often, depending on the size of animal or bird they kill; but their prey is correspondingly more numerous. Probably, however, eagles that live on such small prey that they must kill one or two individuals every day are the exception rather than the rule. Most eagles kill one fairly substantial animal every few days.

On days when they are not hunting, eagles often soar about for a time, and on such days they may mount to great heights with the first good thermals of the day (about 9 A.M. to 10 A.M. in the tropics) or in temperate mountainous lands on updraughts. They probably do not hunt from such great heights, despite their marvellous eyesight. At this time, especially in the tropics, when the air is 'soarable' they very often indulge in nuptial display, even outside the breeding season, perhaps another way in which the pair-bond is maintained. Whether the nest is occupied or not, I can expect to see and hear the male of the pair of Crowned Eagles that lives near my house in nuptial display on any fine morning when the air is soarable, most often between 9.30 and 11.30 A.M. He displays whenever he can, but he must have suitable weather to soar to the great heights at which he can do this; he cannot do it on wet days.

Turning again to Verreaux's Eagles, later in the morning, from 10 A.M. onwards, they will usually be found perched, very often near their nest site, but sometimes on some ledge or tree at a distance from it. Once they have perched in such a position they are probably there for the remainder of the warm part of the day. They sit for hours alert but almost immobile – preening, looking about them indifferently, sometimes making a short flight from one ledge to another. They will not

Wahlberg's Eagle (*Aquila wahlbergi*) – lives mainly on lizards, small mammals and some gamebirds

usually make any more sustained flights till the afternoon.

It is quite likely that this diurnal inactivity on their part is connected with the similar inactivity of the prey (hyrax) and comparable behaviour is shown by many other eagles. In such a case it is difficult to know whether such behaviour is due to inability to catch anything, or merely the heat. When the eagles are not hungry it is presumably due to the heat. In temperate climates this periodicity in the behaviour of eagles is much less marked. A Scottish Golden Eagle may be seen flying about at any hour of the day; it must, for a fine day may be followed by several on which hunting is much more difficult.

If they have fed in the morning, Verreaux's Eagles will be less inclined to take wing again early in the afternoon. But if not, and if they are hungry, they will be more inclined to fly about and hunt. The wind which often rises in tropical countries after midday will also stimulate eagles to fly, as it is then easier for them to soar without effort. Verreaux's Eagles usually take wing again from about 3 A.M. to 6 P.M. In this time they may or may not kill, but they are quite often seen flying about for much of the afternoon even when they are fully fed after a meal in the morning. In such cases they are presumably not flying in order to hunt.

In the evening, the eagles again make their way to their habitual roosting place and settle for the night, perhaps an hour before dark. If they are hungry and have not killed they will fly about till later in the evening, and may, for instance, attack troops of baboons which come to roost on rock ledges late in the evening. In Africa, eagles are seldom seen hunting late in the day; they are more likely to kill in the morning. However, in the case of the Crowned Eagle, I have come across the birds hunting almost in the dusk, when their principal prey – small forest antelopes – are likely to be on the move.

In countries where night and day are almost of equal length Verreaux's Eagles, once settled on their roost perch, remain there for at least twelve, and probably fourteen hours. In Kenya they sometimes spend even longer on the roost. They do not voluntarily fly at night and probably could not see well enough to do so. In temperate countries where the winter nights are very much longer, as for instance in Scotland, a Golden Eagle would be forced to roost from about 3 P.M.

European Sea Eagle (*Haliaëtus albicilla*) – eagles often soar to considerable heights when not hunting

to about 9 A.M. the following day, or at least fifteen hours out of the twenty-four. In summer, *per contra*, the eagle has about twenty hours of adequate daylight in which to fly about and hunt, and may only roost (as opposed to resting briefly on a perch) for about four hours.

The composite picture of an eagle's day that emerges from the observation of Verreaux's Eagle is one where more than half the day is spent roosting, several more hours (perhaps four to six) are spent perching and loafing, and only comparatively short periods, not usually continuous but themselves broken by short periods of perching, are spent in flight. In large eagles, probably a relatively small proportion of the time in flight is spent actively hunting – once every two or three days. It may seem surprising that birds capable of such spectacular feats in flight should spend so much of their time perched; but there it is. Any large eagle is probably able to find prey and kill in rather a short time if necessary, though there may be exceptions.

In some eagles diurnal activity is much easier to observe than in others. Forest eagles are the most difficult, while eagles that normally frequent the waterside are the easiest to watch. One such is the African Fish Eagle, very common on some rivers and lakes of East Africa. It is unlike a large wide-ranging species, such as the Golden or Verreaux's Eagle, in that different pairs may nest only two or three hundred yards apart. The pair then inhabits a very circumscribed area, and their activities can be watched in detail. Moreover, from a boat anchored out in the lake or river, their behaviour could be accurately recorded and later analyzed in detail – not only for one, but for several resident pairs, and any immatures that may be in the area.

If this were done the picture that would emerge is not very different in essentials from that derived from a general observation of Verreaux's Eagle. African Fish Eagles signify that they are awake by calling shortly after dawn, and they may take wing soon after that. Their method of hunting, however, is very different from that of Verreaux's or the Golden Eagle, for it consists of perching on trees and from these making short flights to catch fish. Usually, in such flights, the eagles will only fly a few hundred yards, circling out over the water, and returning to the same or a similar perch. Once again, the pair are often close together and will

Black-breasted Snake Eagle (*Circaëtus pectoralis*) hunting by day. Half the length of the Black-necked Cobra (*Naja nigricollis*) is ingested into the crop

commonly perch on the same tree. When actively hunting they often seem to perceive a fish some distance away, fly straight to it, and make a catch without any difficulty. More rarely they may descend from soaring flight and catch prey well out in the lake. This is particularly true of catfish and lungfish on African lakes, both of which are inclined to come to the surface to breathe at intervals.

Like other eagles African Fish Eagles do not have to kill every day if the fish they catch are large enough to suffice them for more than one meal. They have usually killed before 10 A.M., though sometimes one does see a kill later in the day. The rest of the day is their own, as one might say. When thermals start as the day grows warm they will soar to great heights, attracting attenton to their presence by their ringing call, which is part of their nuptial and territorial display. As the midday heat increases they perch for long periods in the shade of large trees, not again taking wing until the cool of the late afternoon. Although confined to a much smaller area, this general pattern is not very different from that of a wide-ranging eagle such as Verreaux's.

In America, winter populations of migrant Bald Eagles have been observed both by radio-telemetry (with limited success) and by direct observation. The eagles left their roosts soon after dawn and arrived at favourite feeding perches, flying direct, flapping alternating with short glides. They started feeding twenty minutes to half an hour later, making short flights over the water and attempting to catch fish by swooping. Usually any that fed had done so by 10 A.M., only about two hours after dawn. The eagles then flew to other perching areas where they remained inactive in cold dull weather, but on clear fine days with a good wind they usually took to the air and soared about. After soaring about during the afternoon they returned to their roosting sites by degrees, and all were on the roost well before dark. These observations – made in winter in the Mississippi area, in conditions very unlike the equable sunny climate enjoyed by African Fish Eagles at Lake Naivasha, near the equator – demonstrate that an eagle's day does not differ very much in essentials, wherever the eagle happens to be and whatever species of eagle is concerned. More quantitative data are obviously desirable; but it is likely they will confirm results already broadly established by direct observation.

CHAPTER FOUR

Eagles as hunters

It is this aspect of the life of eagles that most interests and affects mankind. The manner in which large and powerful predators catch and kill their victims, while revolting some, is to others a matter for admiration or interest. And if eagles did not hunt and kill other animals and birds that are of some interest to man, they would not affect man's interests in the slightest.

However, hunt and kill they do, in order to survive. And although there are many wonderful tales told of how they do it, and of the size of animals eagles can kill, the number of people who have actually seen and accurately recorded such an incident is small. In a lifetime of watching eagles I myself have seen few kills, and the same is true for others who have spent long periods watching eagles. We know they do kill, and in several species have a very good idea of what they kill, and how often. But precisely how, and especially how they tackle an animal of large size and very considerable strength, is poorly documented.

Before considering the manner of hunting and killing, it will be well to examine some of the physical adaptations for hunting and killing. To start with, consider the eagle's eye: large, brilliant, and proverbially acute. Although I know of no recent detailed study of an eagle's eye, it is probably somewhat similar to that of a buzzard. Eagles' eyes are sometimes brown or dark, but more often have a yellow or bright yellow iris, especially in snake eagles. They are round or globose, and move little in their sockets, so that the eagle

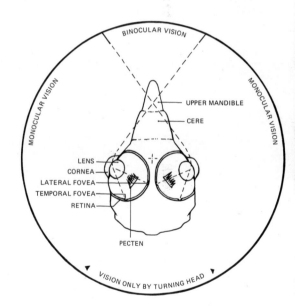

Angle of vision

OPPOSITE: Tawny Eagle (*Aquila rapax*) – the eagle cannot turn its eyes to one side but must turn the whole head

cannot turn its eyes to one side to scan objects, but must move its whole head this way and that. They are directed partly sideways and partly forwards, so that the eagle has good monocular vision on each side, and binocular vision through about thirty-five to fifty degrees of arc in front. Overall visual acuity, as shown by the number of sensitive cells in the retina, is probably about three or four times that of man. However, the eagle's eyes, like those of other large raptors, have two sunken areas on the retina, known as foveas, in which the number of sensitive cells per unit area is greater than in the rest of the retina, and which are centres of still greater visual acuity. One of these foveas is directed forwards, and is used in binocular vision, the other sideways, used in monocular vision with either eye.

There is also a structure called the pecten (from its comb-like appearance) whose function is not clear, but which may cast a shadow on parts of the retina and enable better perception of the shape of objects. The whole apparatus adds up to an eye which probably performs five or six times as well as even our rather acute vision. Where a man sees six indistinguishable rabbits sitting close together like a mass of indeterminate brown fur, the eagle could clearly distinguish all six and take its pick. It is likely that an eagle sees in full colour; but it is possible that some colour perception is sacrificed to obtain greater visual acuity.

Such an eye permits an eagle to detect its prey at long distance, and to resolve the fine detail seen, for instance, when a grouse is hiding in Scottish heather or a well-camouflaged green snake is creeping through tropical vegetation. One may obtain a better idea of what is actually involved by experiment. A human with normal eyesight can see a small object an inch long in a conspicuous position at a range of thirty to thirty-five yards; at greater distances it becomes indistinct. An eagle, with its considerably greater visual acuity could see the same object distinctly at 120 and perhaps at over 200 yards. On the same optical basis, a Scottish Golden Eagle could see a hare, about eighteen inches long when crouched in a feeding posture, at a range of 2,150 yards (a mile and a quarter), and perhaps even at about two miles. Such an eagle, soaring along the ridge of a mountain top should be able to perceive any largish animal incautious enough to move in the whole of a valley two thousand feet below.

Young Crowned Eagle (*Stephanoaëtus coronatus*)

ALULA 1 2 3 4 5

Bending under differential load of emarginated primaries in level soaring flight, so that they lie one above another and act as individual aerofoils at the wing tip

Some eagles, but by no means all, hunt while soaring and most eagles, whether they hunt when soaring or not, soar in an accomplished manner. For efficient soaring an eagle's wing is rather long and broad; it is usually not so broad as that of a vulture, which hunts almost entirely by soaring at a considerable height. The tips of several primaries are emarginated, often on both webs, so that they are widely separated when the wing is fully extended. These widely separated tips act as wing slots, reducing turbulence and increasing efficiency at the end of the wing. They also bend when the eagle is in flight, and lie in different planes (one above another), the foremost long primary being the most bent; this perhaps helps to increase lift at the wingtip as well as reduce turbulence.

When an eagle is in soaring flight, hunting along a ridge from which it can see down into the valley below, it gives an impression of great stability. It does not appear to be jerked about by air currents as is, for instance, a buzzard. This applies especially to large eagles such as Golden Eagles, but is also noticed in such small eagles as Wahlberg's, Ayres', or Booted Eagles, which are no heavier than buzzards. An eagle's apparent stability is thus not only a matter of weight but probably also of wing structure. In a gale that makes it hard for a man to stand, a Scottish Golden Eagle appears almost as steady as the rocks beneath him. When closely watched the eagle's body is almost still; but the wingtips are constantly moving, the spread primaries opening or closing a little every second as the bird makes minute automatic adjustments to the air currents. Such stability evidently is useful to the eagle when hunting. To appreciate the point it is only necessary to think how much more difficult it is to see clearly what is happening when one is being bumped over a rough field in a Landrover than it is when the vehicle is stationary, or when one is travelling in a comfortable Mercedes Benz.

There are various specialized adaptations of the eagle's wing that are connected with hunting in different types of country. Forest eagles, such as the African Crowned and the Harpy, like Sparrowhawks have short and very broad wings,

African Fish Eagle (*Haliaaetus vocifer*) – the widely separated tips of the primaries act as wing slots

Varied wing outlines of eagles:
Golden Eagle: mammal eater, mountains, long wings, rather long tail
Crowned Eagle: mammal eater, forest, short broad wings and long tail
Fish Eagle: fish eater, aquatic, long broad wings, short tail
Bateleur: scavenger/snake eater, continuous soaring, very long wings, very short tail
Martial Eagle: bird-eater, high soarer, savanna, long broad wings, rather short tail

and long tails. The resulting silhouette, typical of almost all hawks that hunt in forests, is probably valuable in making dexterous twists in and out of branches and foliage. The Bateleur Eagle has a long narrow wing that helps it to soar almost continuously over the African plains for many hours at a stretch, at the rather high airspeed of about forty to fifty miles an hour. The Indian Black Eagle has very long, soft, flexible primaries that are not deeply emarginated, but bend freely in flight. This could be an adaptation to assist in very slow flight, which would be useful in detecting the birds' nests and small creatures of the tree-tops of hillsides on which this eagle habitually feeds. Space does not permit a detailed evaluation of all such adaptations even if knowledge on the subject were complete. Suffice it to say that they are many and various, and await critical aerodynamic study.

In whatever way eagles hunt, whether in flight or from a perch, they kill with their feet and feed with the bill. When handling an eagle one does not pay attention to the fierce-looking head but watches the feet, which are what may do damage. Basically the feet of eagles are all rather similar. Three toes are directed forwards (the two outer ones also to the side), and one backwards. The three directed forward are weaker than the one behind, which is equipped with a talon longer and stronger than those on the other toes. The hind claw probably acts as a dagger, piercing the prey, while the three forward claws hold the luckless animal against the hind claw with a clutch of tremendous strength. The force with which a large eagle can grip cannot be understood until one has experienced it, say on one's own fist. When an eagle grips in earnest one's hand becomes numb, and it is quite impossible to tear it free, or to loosen the grip of the eagle's toes with the other hand. One just has to wait till the bird relents, and while waiting one has ample time to realize that an animal such as a rabbit would be very quickly paralyzed, unable to draw breath, and perhaps pierced through and through by the talons in such a clutch.

Eagles kill even the largest prey with their talons. A bush-buck, weighing 35 lbs, killed by a Crowned Eagle had many puncture wounds in its throat. The eagle had evidently landed first on the antelope's back, and then seized the neck with the other foot, killing an animal four time its own weight by strangulation, or perhaps by piercing the spinal column.

The eagle's foot is adapted in various ways according to the type of prey it habitually kills. The feet of fish eagles, which feed on slippery and rather large prey usually caught in water, are equipped with sharp spicules beneath the pads of the toes. Those of snake eagles have short, thick, strong toes which, as one may imagine, grip the slender body of a snake with crushing force and prevent it from slipping through the grasp, as long toes might permit. The feet of the Indian Black Eagle have long claws that are not sharply curved and could not be used effectively for piercing or crushing, but which extend the span of the foot and so perhaps enable the bird to

Golden Eagle (*Aquila chrysaëtos*) – female returning to the nest, note emargination of primaries

OPPOSITE: African Fish Eagle (*Haliaætus vocifer*) – eagles that frequent the waterside are the easiest to watch

ABOVE: Golden Eagle (*Aquila chrysaëtos*) – the widely separated tips of the primaries act as wing slots

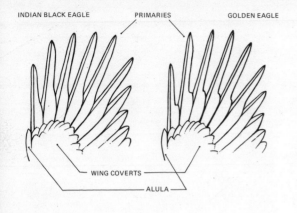

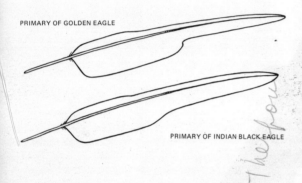

Emargination of primaries to form wing slots; those of the Indian Black Eagle are more flexible and less emarginated than those of the Golden Eagle

snatch in flight a whole bird's nest from which the young or eggs are later extracted.

Most instructive, perhaps, is the sort of comparison that one can make between the feet of two large closely related eagles, such as the Martial and the African Crowned. The Martial Eagle's foot is large, with long rather thin toes at the end of a long leg; ideal, one would suppose, for reaching out to snatch a rapidly moving gamebird, the Martial Eagle's favourite prey. The Crowned Eagle has short, thick, very powerful toes with stout rigid talons, a foot plainly capable of dealing with larger and heavier animals, though the Crowned Eagle is not itself either so large or so heavy as the Martial. The Crowned Eagle's foot is more powerful than that of a Golden Eagle, and will penetrate a falconer's glove, with which a Golden Eagle can be safely handled.

This basic equipment for hunting – of ultra-keen eyesight, an effective soaring wing, and formidable feet – has its limitations. The wing is not designed for extremely swift stoops in flight, such as are practised by the larger falcons, though on occasion eagles do perform swift stoops. The sheer size of large eagles makes them less manoeuvrable, through higher wing-loading, breadth of wingspan and so on; one may see an extremely powerful eagle discomfited by a much smaller bird of prey that it could instantly kill if only it could catch it. The eagle's performance as a hunter is affected by these limitations.

Many eagles do not hunt in flight, but from perches, in this respect resembling buzzards. They may adopt both methods, but spend much more of their time perched than in flight. This is especially true of those eagles that feed upon small, weak, and often cryptically coloured creatures such as rats, lizards, or snakes. Good examples are the African Long-crested Eagle (*Lophaëtus occipitalis*), which feeds almost exclusively on small ground mammals, and spends most of its time perched on trees, or telegraph posts; or the snake eagles that live in forest or woodland, which perch in trees and closely scan the surrounding vegetation for any small movement. The large African Crowned Eagle, which feeds mainly (at least in my experience) on antelopes on the forest floor, catches these by simply dropping on them from a perch not very far above them. But when catching monkeys in the forest canopy it must approach with speed in flight and take these very alert creatures unawares. Fish eagles and sea eagles habitually perch on trees or rocks above the waters they frequent, and very often make their kills from there without difficulty. In Alaska, the Bald Eagle (*Haliætus leucocephalus*) simply stands on the stonebeds and drags dead and dying Pacific salmon from shallow water. But the African Fish Eagle will on occasion catch large fish from soaring flight, with a graceful descent into the water, and will also resort to piracy.

The eagles that hunt mainly in flight are those that live in open country. Differences of habit may even occur between closely related species. For instance, the Brown Snake Eagle (*Circaëtus cinereus*) of Africa hunts mainly from perches in the woodland or thornbush it frequents; but the European Snake Eagle (with its African races, the Black-breasted and Beaudouin's Snake Eagle) inhabits open country and hunts in flight, often hovering with slowly fanning wings like some gigantic kestrel. From the visual viewpoint a hover is equivalent to a stationary perch high up in the air. Many other eagles, such as Golden Eagles, Verreaux's Eagles and Martial Eagles, that live in mountainous or open country, habitually use air-currents rising over mountains to maintain a nearly stationary position over a ridge top. Martial Eagles are in the habit of soaring to greater heights when hunting than are other species of African eagles, and I have seen a Martial Eagle kill a guineafowl from a high soaring pitch at a range of several miles. However, in these species which habitually hunt on the soar, and even more so in other species that live in denser woodland or forest and habitually hunt from perches, it must not be assumed that because the eagle is soaring it is hunting; it may be fully fed, and soaring simply for the sake of soaring.

There are some eagles that hunt by swift flight, something like a combination of falcon and goshawk. These include the small Booted and Ayres' Hawk-eagles, and probably the Rufous-bellied Hawk-eagle of India (*Hieraaëtus kienerii*). They feed largely on birds, which they catch either in open country or in dense woodland by very swift stoops. In Spain I watched a Booted Eagle stoop with terrific force at a Red-legged Partridge, from a height of more than five hundred feet; it missed the partridge, which escaped. In Kenya I have watched a soaring Ayres' Hawk-eagle suddenly close its wings and plunge into the treetops with falcon-like speed, to emerge a little further away with a bird in its talons. In such a case one

Harpy Eagle (*Harpia harpyja*) – in the wild this species lives in forests; the broad wings and long tail are probably valuable in making dexterous twists in and out of branches

must assume that the soaring eagle saw the bird in the tree-tops before beginning its stoop, and knew these trees sufficiently well to be able to dash swiftly through them to catch its prey; but it is possible that such stoops into the treetops are often made and that birds are collected as and when possible. This method of hunting, so far as I know, is almost unique, for falcons that perform these swift stoops do not do so into cover, and goshawks that habitually catch birds in cover do not soar above the trees first.

With a few exceptions, when I have been lucky enough to see an eagle kill its prey, it has been rather a prosaic matter. On one occasion, when I watched a Golden Eagle kill, the prey was something very small and feeble, probably a young curlew. The eagle descended gently from low soaring flight, alighted, and seized the small object, which she swallowed in two gulps. On many occasions I have seen Long-crested Eagles lean forward suddenly on their telegraph poles, drop into the grass immediately below them, and seize a rat; no great skill or even dexterity is required here. Tawny Eagles, likewise, kill burrowing mole rats in Africa with great ease, and habitually prey on them. But Tawny Eagles can also kill flamingoes high up in the air, with a swift falcon-like stoop.

African Fish Eagles and their relatives usually snatch a fish from the water surface, apparently without difficulty. But I have seen one descend gently from soaring flight to catch a large fish a mile or so away offshore. Fifty feet above the water, it raised its wings high, so accelerating the speed of the descent, and plunged with a splash to fix its talons in the fish's back. It then lay on the surface with wings spread for a minute or so, then flapped forwards, 'oaring' across the surface with its wings, until finally airborne, the fish clasped in the talons fore and aft like a torpedo beneath an aircraft. The fish was too heavy for the eagle to rise easily and it flapped along, gathering speed, until it was finally able to swoop up onto a perch.

In Scotland I was once watching a female Golden Eagle, off her nest in the evening. She was soaring above a wide glen, and was about two miles from me and perhaps 1,000 feet above the floor of the glen. Suddenly she closed her wings and plunged vertically to the ground, disappearing behind a fold of the hill so that I could not see whether she killed or not. Her speed of descent was so immediate and so great that it

Booted Eagle (*Hieraaëtus pennatus*) – note three toes are directed forwards (the two outer also to the side) and one backwards; the hind claw probably acts as a dagger piercing the prey, while the forward claws clutch it with tremendous strength

OPPOSITE: Crowned Eagle (*Stephanoaëtus coronatus*) – on a kill in Nairobi National Park

OVERLEAF: *left* Booted Eagle (*Hieraaëtus pennatus*) – at the nest; it hunts either in open country or dense woodland by very swift stoops, feeding largely on birds
right Bateleur Eagle (*Terathopius ecaudatus*) – male incubating, nest thirty feet above ground in *Ficus sycamorus*

seemed hardly possible that it was entirely due to gravity, and she must have been very close to the ground when she disappeared. I have also seen Scottish Golden Eagles make spectacular swift stoops at a herring gull and once at a cuckoo, missing the object of the attack by a few inches at speed. It is impossible to believe that in such cases the eagle could not have killed the bird if it wished; and we must assume that it did not wish to and that these attacks were in the nature of play. In his book on the Golden Eagle, Seton Gordon records many instances of Golden Eagles attacking at speed, and on occasion killing on the wing.

When eagles such as Golden Eagles attack large animals – deer for instance – the latter are usually either weak or disabled. Seton Gordon recounts a number of instances, culled from his numerous acquaintances among the Highland stalkers. These include attacks made upon deer calves, or upon sheep trapped among rocks, or even attempts to drive deer over cliffs. There is a great danger of misinterpretation here, for such large eagles will stoop in play at an animal, such as a leopard or grizzly bear, which they could not by any stretch of the imagination kill; but it is quite possible that an eagle driven by hunger would attack a disabled or weakened adult deer. I myself have seen a half-grown hind fall over a cliff in spring from sheer weakness, to land almost at my feet with a broken back; had an eagle been soaring near her an observer might well have assumed that her fall had something to do with the eagle.

On occasions, however, large and powerful eagles will attack perfectly healthy animals very much larger than themselves, and so strong that a man could hardly hold them. The Crowned Eagles that live in the forest near my home sometimes kill young bushbuck. One such animal, already mentioned, was a young male that must have weighed thirty-five pounds; and another, almost as large, was the subject of a tremendous struggle. I found the eagle on the kill and reconstructed the incident from the signs. The eagle had dropped on the bushbuck as it was walking out into a glade along a track through thick shrubs. The bushbuck had then leapt three or four yards to the right, where it had been downed. There was a large area of flattened vegetation here where the bushbuck had struggled and its flailing legs had broken the bushes. However the eagle had evidently killed, plucked, and

Bones collected below the nest of a Crowned Eagle (*Stephanoaëtus coronatus*) including: *top left* leg of impala calf and backbone of a duiker; *centre top* two skulls of suni (*Nesotragus moschatus*), two skulls of hyrax and part of skull of immature bushbuck; *top right* long arm-bone of a large primate (probably Colobus monkey) and leg bones of antelopes; *lower left* pelvic girdles of suni; *lower centre* skull of water mongoose (*Atilax paludinosus*) and two monkey skulls; *bottom centre* assorted pelvic and jaw-bones of suni

dismembered the bushbuck at this spot, which was strewn with hair. The four legs and the head had been dissected from the body and removed elsewhere, and the body itself had then been torn in half at the middle of the backbone. These two pieces the eagle had dragged down a ten-yard long bush tunnel (in which she had defecated) to a shady open space beneath the tree from which she had probably launched the attack. Here I found her feeding while her mate was also in the area. Next day each brought a leg of bushbuck to the nest, a mile-and-a-half away, proving that these had been cached

European Serpent Eagle (*Circaëtus gallicus*) – the water snake caught by the male has just been passed to the female before being offered to the chick

European Serpent Eagle (*Circaëtus gallicus*) – a hover, from the visual viewpoint, is the equivalent of a stationary perch

somewhere in the forest. Despite the evidence of the struggle that had flattened the vegetation over a large area, the eagle had lost only one breast feather and a few flecks of down.

That eagles can kill animals three or four times their own weight is therefore definite. Probably, however, such occasions are rare. More often they kill animals half their own weight or less, of a size more convenient to carry. To be able to carry away prey quickly is an advantage as, when on the ground – especially in forest – an eagle is vulnerable to other predators.

Many eagles that are perfectly capable of killing large and active animals will feed on carrion, or upon small and helpless creatures when they have the chance. Golden Eagles habitually eat carrion in winter both in Scotland and America, and African Fish Eagles that skilfully kill large fish in open water can also be seen hopping from nest to nest in a heronry, gobbling the young. Some of the eagles that feed upon carrion also resort to piracy. These include the Fish and Sea Eagles, the Tawny Eagle, and the Bateleur – none closely related to one another, but all inclined to eat carrion as well as live prey. Probably piracy is associated with the carrion-eating habit.

Piracy, as I have seen it performed by Tawny Eagles, Fish Eagles and Bateleurs, involves robbing other birds of their prey, or of pieces of carrion they may have taken. I have watched a Bateleur fly at and buffet a passing vulture, returning to the attack time after time with great force, though it obtained no reward. I have seen Tawny Eagles pursue and rob birds much smaller than themselves, and have also seen them pursue an adult Martial Eagle with success, and a Lammergeier without success. Fish Eagles habitually attempt to pirate the kills of other fish-eating birds, and I have seen them take fish or frogs from Ospreys, Hammerkops and herons, and unsuccessfully attempt to do so from the very formidable Saddle-billed Stork and Goliath Heron. Recently I watched a pair of Fish Eagles, entirely surrounded by flamingoes they could easily have caught, pursue a couple of Yellow-billed Storks relentlessly for two miles or more, a much more sustained and vigorous flight than is usually undertaken by any Fish Eagle. The attacks in this case were unsuccessful. Doubtless the storks may have had frogs, but though both were eventually overtaken and forced to the ground, they disgorged none and the Fish Eagles returned empty-handed.

Thus, although eagles are very formidably equipped, and can on occasion use their armament with spectacular effect, they usually kill well within their strength, and will help themselves to the weak, helpless, or dead individuals among their habitual prey when they can. Admittedly much more needs to be learned by direct observation about the methods used by eagles to kill, but this generalization is probably correct.

Even when knowledge is much more complete than it is today, it will probably turn out that eagles normally kill by dexterity – if that – rather than by spectacular speed or strength; also, that the majority of what they kill is well within their powers and that the many exaggerated accounts of their rapacity and ferocity are nonsense.

African Fish Eagle (*Haliaætus vocifer*) – feeding with vultures on carrion (elephant's trunk)

CHAPTER FIVE

Eagles at home

It is well known that in many species of eagles a nest site is occupied for many years, sometimes for generations. Any actual nest may be abandoned, or may fall down, but others will be built on the same cliff, in the same tree, or close by. This constancy is sometimes recorded in place names. In Scotland, cliffs where the Golden Eagle is habitually seen, or where it sometimes nests, are often called 'Creag na'h Iolaire' – the Eagle's Crag. Place names may even locate an apparently unsuitable breeding site. Once in Scotland I had thoroughly searched a series of likely corries, without result. There were eagles in the area, for I saw them. I was about to give it up, and reconcile myself to the fact that the nest had escaped even my own experienced and keen vision, when another look at the ordnance map revealed a small burn called 'Allt an Fhir Eoin', which may be translated 'Water of the Man Bird.' Only one species could possibly be a 'man bird' in Scotland, and though the burn looked thoroughly unpromising, investigation revealed a little gully with a thirty-foot cliff, a sheltered, overhung ledge, and an eaglet in a nest obviously of long standing and undoubtedly known to those who compiled the names on the map almost a century before.

Such constancy at the nest site is not invariable among eagles, and appears to depend primarily on the species, and secondly, on the size of the eagle concerned. Sea and fish eagles make huge nests, and stick to them year after year; so do the larger eagles with feathered tarsi, for instance the genera *Aquila*, *Stephanoaëtus*, and *Polemaëtus*. The same seems

Crowned Eagle (*Stephanoaëtus coronatus*) – this nest is probably fifty years old

OPPOSITE: Golden Eagle (*Aquila chrysaëtos*) one of the species that is constant to a nest site, sometimes for generations

63

OPPOSITE: Brown Snake Eagle (*Circaëtus cinereus*) – female at nest with one egg in *Acacia nigriscens*

ABOVE: Golden Eagle (*Aquila chrysaëtos*) – about two weeks old

OPPOSITE: *above* Black-breasted Snake Eagle
(*Circaëtus pectoralis*) – flimsy nest, barely visible
in the crown of a *Euphorbia* among thornbush
below Eggs of the Golden Eagle (*Aquila
chrysaëtos*) lying on a bed of freshly plucked
Greater Woodrush (*Luzula sylvatica*)

to be true of Harpy Eagles in Guyana, and Philippine
Monkey-eaters, though very little has been recorded of these
or related birds in this respect.

Not all eagles, however, make large nests, or stick to the
same places year after year. Tawny Eagles, for instance, often
use a nest for only one year, though I have known sites occupied for up to six years. Snake eagles, even the largest ones
such as the Brown Snake Eagle, make small, well-concealed
flimsy nests of thin sticks in the crowns of acacias or euphor-
bias, and move so often that one must reckon to locate them
anew each year; they may move a few hundred yards, or
several miles. In due time, after a lapse of many years, a
Snake Eagle may again use the same euphorbia; but by then
the individuals of the pair are probably different, and the
same tree may be selected because it is, for some reason,
attractive to Snake Eagles. Bateleurs are an exception to this
rule of frequent moving among Snake Eagles; they build a
larger, more solid nest than most, usually in an acacia, and
use it for several years in succession. I have even known a
Bateleur to use the same acacia between 1951 and 1968,
though what made this tree attractive among thousands of
others is obscure.

Smaller eagles, even when closely related to much larger
species (which do stick to the same site), do not necessarily
use the same nest year after year. Wahlberg's Eagle (in the
same genus as the Golden Eagle) usually has one to three
nests close to each other in the same general area; but the nest
site is moved from time to time. I have followed the gradual
progression of one pair of Wahlberg's Eagles from 1949 to
1968; in that time they have had, to my knowledge, a total
of six nests in four different sites, the greatest distance between
the sites being about two-and-a-half miles, with other sites in
between. All of these nests were, however, in the same broad
valley, or its tributaries, so that the same territory was occupied
by successive birds.

A few eagles seem to occupy a nest area for several years in
succession, then unaccountably move away for several miles.
One such is the African Hawk-eagle, which builds nests in
large trees in the savanna. One pair known to me occupied
the same hill from 1950 to 1957 without a break, then moved
for no apparent reason. Although I had no proof, I suspected
that this pair 'reappeared' about three miles away a year or

Sketch map of movements of a pair of
Wahlberg's Eagles between 1949 and 1968.
The eagles moved gradually downstream
along one watercourse, then crossed to
another, but all in the same general drainage
area.
Dotted contour lines indicative only. Figures
on base line show approximate scale in miles

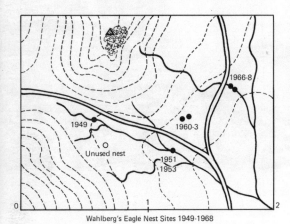

1966-8

1949

Unused nest

1960-3

1951
1953

0   1   2

Wahlberg's Eagle Nest Sites 1949-1968

so later, in an area that up till then had not held a pair of African Hawk-eagles, and which they occupied up till 1968.

What causes these changes to take place is obscure; but it is a good general rule to search first for eagles' nests where they have been known before, and to look further afield only when this area has been thoroughly searched. Whenever I have made a population study of eagle in any tract of country I have found that this rule of definite predictable spatial relationship applies. Locate one nest, and then, with almost mathematical precision, one can forecast where another is likely to be. Nests may be one, four, or even ten miles apart, or in African Fish-eagles, only two to three hundred yards; but these distances are regular, as will appear when they are plotted on a map. However suitable the nest sites in the intervening country, one may search till one is blue in the face without finding anything. But a few minutes search in a 'likely' area, perhaps no more than a mile square, will very often reveal the nests perhaps on a ledge or tree apparently much less suitable than unoccupied sites in the intervening country. However, if there is no suitable crag or tree, one cannot expect to find an eagle, even where one ought to be, on a spatial basis.

In practice eagles occupy a territory or home range that does not vary much from year to year. 'Territory' is a bad term since it normally implies a defended area, and most eagles do not obviously defend the areas they live in; 'home range' is preferable. The actual nest site may be moved within it a few hundred yards or a mile. Of three Martial Eagles known to me from 1949 to 1968, one moved its nest site about a mile in 1952, and was still using the same nest in 1968; a second had moved about a mile some time between 1956 and 1966; and the third built a new nest in 1965 a hundred yards from the old one. Such moves may be connected with a change of mate – a new female may not like the old nest and may want to build a new one – or with frequent disasters. Among Golden Eagles in Sutherland I found in 1967 that well-known pairs that were liable to frequent human disturbance had on the average more nests than those which nested in remote areas. By building a small new nest on an obscure ledge a Golden Eagle that is regularly disturbed may evade egg-collectors who know of all the old sites.

In the case of eagles that move their nests frequently, such as snake eagles, perhaps the home range is also movable, though this aspect has not been studied. It is in any case extremely difficult to establish boundaries for any eagle's range. In eagles such as the Golden Eagle where the same nest site continues to be occupied, if undisturbed, for many years, the home range presumably remains the same, but is occupied by a succession of different birds. As already mentioned, it is not necessary for Golden Eagles to live much more than ten years in the wild state to rear enough young to replace themselves. So, when a home range is occupied for

Wahlberg's Eagle (*Aquila wahlbergi*) – a small nest, the site will not be occupied for more than a decade

half a century or more, there must have been several generations of adults in that time. This is not adequately confirmed by direct observation in Golden Eagles; but in the African Crowned Eagle, another species that builds a huge nest and occupies it for many years, observed changes of mate (easily recognizable in this boldly marked species) have shown that the nest is occupied by a succession of individual birds.

At one Crowned Eagle nest site, now in its twentieth year of continuous observation, there have been two males and three females since 1949. One male, Rex II, is still alive and well, although at least fifteen years old. One female, Regina II, lived at the site from 1952–61, breeding regularly every second year and feeding the still dependent young in the alternate years. Her successor, Regina III, presumably would not feed her predecessor's offspring and bred when she first arrived in 1961. She began by being unusually prolific for this species, laying a replacement clutch in one year. In the last three years, however, possibly because she has now gone blind in her right eye (making her easier to recognize), she has failed to rear young—though she can still fly about normally. The Ayres' Hawk-eagles that nest not far away have had more frequent changes of mates, particularly among the females. The first two females were relatively successful but latterly, probably because of a series of disasters, the breeding success by three females has been poor.

An eagle's nest is constructed by both members of the pair, but often the female remains in the structure while the male brings nesting material. In a pair of Crowned Eagles near my house, the nest may be added to at almost any time of the year. But there are peak periods of building, at the onset of each nesting cycle, when the male and female are at the site almost every day. Sometimes, too, the female builds up the nest when the male is away, and when an eaglet is in the nest she brings many green branches. This nest was begun in 1959; it is, and will be for many years, very much smaller than the huge nest at Eagle Hill, in Embu District, which I have known from 1949 to 1969, and which has changed little in

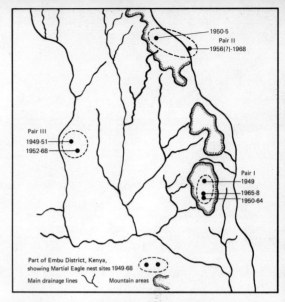

Regular spacing of Martial Eagle breeding sites.

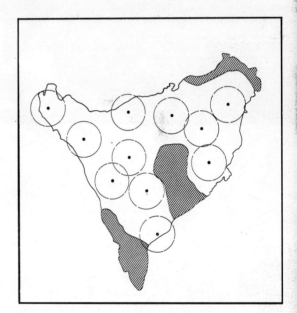

Regular spacing of eleven breeding sites in an area of Scotland of Golden Eagle (*Aquila chrysaëtos*). The circles represent a radius of two miles. The shaded areas are unsuitable for breeding eagles

OPPOSITE: Crowned Eagle (*Stephanoaëtus coronatus*) – Rex II at nest with ninety-day old eaglet

ABOVE: Young Imperial Eagle (*Aquila heliaca*) an 'innocent' species much persecuted by man

Crowned Eagle (*Stephanoaëtus coronatus*).
Although a large eagle, Rex II is dwarfed by
the nest which is six ft across by eight ft deep.
This male is at least fourteen to fifteen years
old

that time. It must obviously have been occupied for many
years before I found it, having been much larger in 1949 than
the one near my house is in 1969, ten years after it was begun.

Eagles build their nests of sticks, heather, seaweed, or any
available material. They break off dead or living branches, or
pick up dead sticks, carrying large ones in the feet, small twigs
in the bill. On cliff ledges they often start with a relatively
small scrape, round which sticks are placed. In time, such a
nest grows into a tower-like structure if head room is un-
limited, or if under an overhang, may spread along the ledge.
Individual eagles vary in the amount of material they add
from year to year, and the same pair may build the nest more
in one year than another. One eagle may add only a few
sticks before laying, while another may extensively build up
one, or even several, alternative nests, and not lay in any of
them when the time comes. Normally, there is a peak of
building activity just before egg laying, at least in countries
where the weather conditions do not limit this activity. In
Scotland, a nest of the Golden Eagle may be built mainly in
the summer slack time, when there are no young in the nest,
and not used till later. In Sutherland, in May and June of
1967, I found several Golden Eagles that had no young building up nests or making new ones; those that still had young
in the nest were otherwise busy and had no time to spare for
building. I have also seen Golden Eagles building steadily in
August and September, and Seton Gordon has recorded
building activity in winter.

Perhaps this apparent compulsion to build at odd times
when they can, helps to keep eagles constant to the nest site.
Materials are added to the nest through the breeding season
as well, the bringing of a green spray often being associated
with copulation, nest relief, or when food is brought. Female
eagles, in particular, bring many green branches to the nest
when there is a young bird in it. The young may not need to
be fed or brooded, but still need to be guarded, and so the
female perches for hours on a branch or ledge near by. From
time to time – as if to relieve monotony – she collects a green
branch or sprig of heather and brings it to the nest. When the
male appears with food she too may come to the nest with a
green branch. An apparent compulsion to build may help to
keep the female near the nest site, where she is needed, instead
of going away to hunt, which could expose the eaglet to

danger. This is, at any rate, a more likely reason for bringing green branches than aesthetic pleasure in adorning the nest, or shading the eaglet from the sun, as sometimes suggested.

Many, but not all, eagles have several alternate nest sites in their range. I have never known a Crowned Eagle to have more than one nest, and the same applies to most Martial Eagles. Verreaux's Eagles usually have from one to three nests, and Scottish Golden Eagles one to eight, usually two or three. (The average in Sutherland is 2·35 per pair.) When there are many nests, it may be partly due to frequent interference. Smaller eagles such as the African Hawk-eagle, or its nominate European race, Bonelli's Eagle, have two or three. A nest is likely to be more durable when placed on a cliff than in a tree, where storms or the rotting of a branch may dislodge it completely. Most eagles, however, nest in trees, and the nests often last for a long time. Snake eagles probably have only one nest in use at a time, and any alternatives have probably been abandoned; but African Fish Eagles, like the larger true eagles, have one to four nests which they will use in rotation.

It has often been suggested that alternative sites are necessary because the nest in use in any year becomes so foul that it cannot be used in a successive year. I do not know of any real evidence to support this contention, and it appears that Golden Eagles with only one nest use it year after year just as successfully as those that use several alternatives. This question needs more critical study. In the tropics, the nest is usually washed clean by the rainy season in between periods of use, and perhaps building new nests may have more to do with changes of mates, or interference, or disasters, than the avoidance of parasites. A Golden Eagle's nest in summer does become rather a foul mess of decaying bones and flies, but in the tropics eagles' nests are never, in my experience, so foul.

When the nest has been made ready by adequate building the female may lay her eggs, or she may not. Eagles invariably lay small clutches, and may lay only one; this applies to very small eagles, such as Ayres' Eagle or Wahlberg's, as much as to large species such as the Martial Eagle. Many eagles lay two eggs, sometimes one or three; very rarely have more than three been recorded. An eagle that lays one egg one year may lay two in another, as did one Crowned Eagle, Regina II, at Eagle Hill. Where there are two or more eggs they are laid at intervals of several days, which affects the survival of

Nest of European Sea Eagle (*Haliaætus albicilla*)

73

the chicks, as incubation always begins with the laying of the first egg.

In most eagles only the female incubates, but males often do so too, especially when a male has brought food for the female and she leaves the nest to eat it. The male may then take a spell on the eggs, lasting from ten minutes or less to several hours. Females sometimes depend almost entirely on the male for food when they are incubating; but do not seem to have large appetites, and are not fed every day by their mates. Some females, for instance in the Golden Eagle, may leave the nest to feed; and it is possible, though not proven, that they may then either go straight to carrion or may perhaps encounter the male with prey near the nest. When both sexes incubate the female may also feed the male on the remnants of any kill she makes when off the nest.

The incubation period is usually long, no matter what the size of the eagle. In those cases where adequate data exist – which does not, for instance, apply to any of the South American Harpy-like eagles – the periods recorded are from forty-two to forty-nine days. The very small Ayres' Eagle incubates for forty-five days, and Wahlberg's for forty-six, whereas a Golden Eagle, twice their size and four times their weight, or more, incubates from forty-three to forty-five days. Snake Eagles may have very long incubation periods, of fifty days or perhaps even more.

Not every eagle lays eggs every year. Non-breeding is frequent, particularly among tropical eagles, but it is also known among Golden Eagles in Scotland. The causes are obscure, but have almost certainly nothing to do with the food supply, at least in the early part of the breeding season. In Scotland in March, when the Golden Eagle lays, there is readily available carrion in abundance, in the shape of dead deer or sheep, lying about in the hills. At Lake Naivasha in Kenya, a recent study of Fish Eagles indicates that only about two-thirds of the known pairs may breed in the course of a year, though fish are so abundant and so easily caught that food shortage is barely conceivable.

It is possible that it is not shortage of food as such, but of the right sort of food, presented in the right way, that may inhibit laying by the female eagle. If, for instance, it were necessary for a female Golden Eagle to be fed on fresh grouse by the male, for psychological or physiological reasons, she might not

74

be able to lay even in years when there was abundant sheep and deer carrion available. However, it is difficult to see how such a consideration could affect African Fish Eagles at Lake Naivasha, where fresh food is perennially abundant, and much more observation is needed. What may certainly be said is that even when a pair regularly occupies a territory and builds up nests they may not succeed in laying eggs, and that this is probably not due to actual food shortage.

At any nest site, a pair of eagles remains mated for the life of any one member of the pair. This is clearly true in those few species whose nests have been observed for long enough to provide the necessary evidence, though again, much more data is needed generally to prove the point. On pages 76 and 77 I have set out the observed changes of mate in two pairs of Crowned Eagles and one pair of Ayres' Eagles, observed for twenty, ten, and nineteen years respectively. When a male or a female disappears from the home range the survivor does not pine, but remains near the nest, and in due course another bird is attracted. Sometimes such a bird may be an immature, or a sub-adult; I have seen pairs of African Fish Eagles composed of a sub-adult and an adult, displaying and performing all the usual functions, and pairs made up of two sub-adults. However, in all these cases an adult later replaced the sub-adult, indicating that a full adult is preferred if available, even when the preliminaries of pair-formation have already been performed with another younger individual. This is yet another example of constancy to the territory – and to the nest site, which is the guiding principle of the lives of eagles at home – as opposed to the individuals making up a pair.

ABOVE: Imperial Eagle (*Aquila heliaca*) at nest
BELOW: African Hawk-eagle (*Hieraaëtus fasciatus spilogaster*) male incubating in untidy newly made nest; this species normally nests in trees

Changes of mates and breeding attempts in two pairs of Crowned and one pair of Ayres' eagles

CROWNED EAGLE

31 Nest years
18 Attempts including one relaying
4 Failures
14 Young reared = 0·45 young/pair/annum
3 male changes (one forced) and two female changes in thirty-one years, average one every 6·2 years

AYRES' EAGLE

19 Nest years
14 Attempts to breed including one relaying
4 Failures
10 Young reared = 0·54 young/pair/annum
1 male change and four female changes in nineteen years, or one every 3·8 years

The male Crowned Eagle at Karen was killed in the prime of life in November 1968

Year	Crowned Eagle at Eagle Hill		Crowned Eagle at Karen		Ayres' Hawk-Eagle at Eagle Hill	
	Male	Female	Male	Female	Male	Female
1949		Laid; failed				
1950		Reared one young				Reared one young
1951		Young dependent; did not breed				Reared one young
1952		Reared one young				Reared one young
1953		Young dependent; did not breed				Reared one young
1954		Reared one young				Reared one young
1955		Young dependent; did not breed				Reared one young
1956		Reared one young				Reared one young
1957		Young dependent; did not breed				Reared one young
1958		Reared one young		Pair present; did not breed		Laid; failed
1959		Young dependent; did not breed		Built nest; reared one young		Reared one young
1960		Reared one young		Young dependent; did not breed		Did not breed

Year	Territory 1	Territory 2	Territory 3
1961	Reared one young	Reared one young	Did not breed
1962	Young dependent; did not breed	Young dependent; did not breed	Laid; failed. Relaid
1963	Laid twice. Reared one young	New male; did not breed	Reared one young
1964	Young dependent; did not breed	Reared one young	Laid; failed
1965	Reared one young	Young dependent; did not breed	Did not breed
1966	Young died? Laid November; failed	Reared one young which died before independence	Did not breed
1967	Laid; failed. Female blind right eye	Laid December	Laid; failed
1968	Did not breed	Reared one young. Male killed. Young dependent	Did not breed

Male Rex I pre 1949-57 Rex II 1958-68 on Female Regina I pre 1949-52 Regina II 1952-60 Regina III 1961-8 on	Male Blackie pre 1958-62 No name 1963-8 when killed Female Loosefeather pre 1959-68 on	Male William pre 1950-7 Old Whitey 1958-68 on Female Mary I pre 1950-c 1954 Mary II c 1954/5-59 Quicksilver 1959-64 Anne 1964-7

Footnote: Crowned Eagle at Kenya. May 1969: Lolita, young of Blackie and Loosefeather, became independent and mated with Sambo, a very dark coloured eagle. Possibly son of Blackie as only two such black eagles of this species. Loosefeather not seen since June 1969.

77

CHAPTER SIX

The young eagle

Since it is much easier to watch eagles at the nest than else-where, they have been more closely studied there than away from it. As a general rule one ought not to try to observe or photograph eagles at close range when they have eggs. But once they have young they are usually relatively easy to observe from a hide or blind at close quarters. When small eaglets are in the nest there is the best chance of seeing the adults and observing them at close range. As a result, we have a pretty good idea of the behaviour of several species at the nest, and especially of the growth and behaviour of the eaglets, which are often doing something amusing or interest-ing even when the adults are not there.

The interval of several days between the laying of the first and subsequent eggs, in cases where more than one is laid, means that the first hatched eaglet (known for convenience as C.1) is several times the size of the second one hatched (C.2) when the latter emerges from the shell. In the Golden Eagle the hatching weight is about three-and-a-half ounces (100 grams). Three young (the third having just hatched), weighed twelve-and-a-half, nine, and three-and-a-half ounces (357, 252 and 98 grams). The first hatched, C.1, then about six days old, was not twice as heavy as the second hatched, C.2; but C.2 was more than twice as heavy as the third hatch-ed, C.3. This is the significant difference between the new hatched chick and a three day old one; the smallest chick died.

Lesser Spotted Eagle (*Aquila pomarina*) – the second chick is never reared

OPPOSITE: Golden Eagle (*Aquila chrysaëtos*) – 'Cain and Abel' battle between two eaglets, the elder attacking the younger

African Hawk-eagle (*Hieraaëtus fasciatus spilogaster*) – a pair with two young; the male (left) is slighter and smaller than the female

A newly hatched eaglet is a weak and feeble little creature that cannot raise its heavy head on its rather thin neck, cannot see properly through partly closed eyes, and must be continuously brooded by its parent. It may not take any nourishment for twenty-four to forty-eight hours after hatching, and when it does must be very carefully and gently induced to feed by the powerful parent. The parent tears off shreds of red flesh from prey and holds them out to the eaglet, on the tip of the hooked bill. The eaglet, which like other birds of prey is inclined to peck at anything red, pecks at the flesh and so takes its first small meal. If the eaglet cannot be induced to feed it will die; it cannot be force-fed by the parent.

When only one eaglet hatches, all goes smoothly and the eaglet has no competition for whatever food may be available. However, when there are two eggs, C.1 is sitting up, taking nourishment, and rapidly becoming more active, while C.2, just hatched, is weak and feeble. A most extraordinary battle to the death commonly develops between the two chicks, often referred to as the 'Cain and Abel battle'. The end result is that the elder usually kills the younger eaglet, so that only one survives.

The battle is usually initiated by the elder chick, which pecks at the younger; but it may sometimes be started by C.2, apparently bent on suicide, for the much stronger C.1 at once retaliates, and usually continues the fight long after C.2 has turned away and tried to escape. The posture of the attacking eaglet is one of threat display – head raised to the full length of the neck, wings partly spread, squatting on its tarsi; at a later stage it will use the same attitude to intimidate any possible enemy. C.1 pursues C.2 around the nest, sometimes for hours, pecking at its exposed back, and squatting on it. Once it has made a wound, it may hack repeatedly at that place. It utters sharp fierce-sounding cries all the time, and C.2 responds with shrill squeals of unavailing protest. If the parents are present they do nothing at all to interfere; and usually C.1 kills C.2 within a day or two of steady attacks. The little body lies on the nest until it is removed, and though this is not proven, it is probably eaten by the parents, or is fed to the victorious C.1.

It has sometimes been suggested that the victor is most often a female, because among birds of prey, females are usually larger and fiercer than males. However, this is incorrect; it is the elder eaglet which kills the younger, and available evidence suggests that a male is just as likely to survive this battle as a female. Perhaps if a female hatches second, her growth rate might be slightly faster than that of a male, so that she might have a better chance of surviving his attacks than vice-versa. But the essential feature is that C.1, when C.2 hatches, is at least twice the weight of, and very much more active than its sibling, so that the outcome of the battle is more or less predetermined, whether C.2 fights back vigorously or not. It is as unequal a contest as one between a strong and active heavyweight boxer and a lightweight just out of a hospital bed.

Young Wahlberg's Eagle (*Aquila wahlbergi*) aged two weeks
BELOW: The same bird aged two months

Young Brown Snake Eagle (*Circaëtus cinereus*) swallowing snake unaided; the feathers of the upperparts develop earlier than the underparts and tail

In many species where this battle occurs, the result is invariable; the second young bird is never reared. This applies, for instance, to the Lesser and Greater Spotted Eagles, to Verreaux's Eagle, and the Crowned Eagle. In some other species, for instance the Tawny Eagle, Golden Eagle and African Hawk Eagle, C.1 kills C.2 in about four cases in five. In Sea Eagles and Fish Eagles the young fight less vigorously and there is a better chance that both will be reared; sometimes even three are reared from three eggs. This difference in behaviour between sea and true eagles with feathered tarsi is more likely to be genetic than anything to do with food supply. The overall effect of this battle is to eliminate the younger chick in about nine cases in ten.

The evolutionary significance of this battle is obscure; it has puzzled all those who have studied its effects. What is curious about it is that it is apparently wasteful. Two eggs are laid, usually two hatch, but the potential reproductive rate is then reduced within a few days by almost half, through this battle alone. Such battles are not confined to eagles – they occur, for instance, among some cranes which lay small clutches, and young herons fiercely attack one another in the nest. Many other birds of prey, but not all (not, for instance, sparrowhawks and harriers), have their breeding potential sharply reduced very early in the fledging period by this fratricidal strife.

Various explanations have been advanced for this behaviour, but none is very satisfactory. One is that survival of the elder chick is directly related to better food supply, for even if both survive, the elder and larger will normally be fed first if it is hungry and begs. Although there is evidence, for instance in the Golden Eagle in Scotland, that brood survival is slightly better in areas of good than of poor food supply, abundance of food is not the whole explanation. The battle still takes place, and the younger chick is eliminated, even when the nest is full of food; moreover the appetite of the chicks is so small at this stage compared to what it will be six weeks later, that actual shortage of food is improbable. Another explanation is that when food is likely to be short the parents deliberately withhold food from the younger chick. This will not do either; there is no observed evidence to that effect, and the parents take no interest in the strife. One possible explanation is that advanced by E. G. Rowe for Verreaux's Eagle – that in the presence of a possibly competitive nest mate, C.1 is stimulated to take more food than it would if it were alone, and so gets a better start in life. Although this is based on actual observations, it needs confirmation by more evidence. It seems best at present to admit that the evolutionary value of this battle is obscure; but one may suggest that it is perhaps merely the exercise of aggressiveness between the chicks, in which the weaker inevitably perishes.

The survivor of the battle, or a single eaglet, grows rapidly. Clad in thin down when it is hatched, it grows a second, longer and thicker coat of down after two to three weeks; once it has this second coat it requires less brooding, and is mainly covered by the parent at night, or in wet cold weather. Feathers begin to come through the body down at ages varying from 20–40 days, according to the size of the eaglet; later in the larger species. Once the feathers have appeared they quickly cover the down, and the eaglet can then be left alone, unbrooded, in the nest. In snake eagles, which breed in very open nests on the tops of trees, fully exposed to the sun, the feathers of the head, neck and back develop more rapidly than do the tail and underparts, probably an adaptation to the exposure of an open site. In most other species, however, the head looks downy after the back and wings are feathered.

Up to the feathering stage the eaglet must normally be fed by the parents; usually by the female only, though males will occasionally do so. The male usually brings prey, the female stays on or near the nest, brooding or guarding the eaglet. The killing rate of the male, in several species, notably the Crowned Eagle, is more than doubled immediately after the hatch. At this stage he feeds himself, his mate, and the eaglet or eaglets, and the frequency with which he kills is evidently not governed solely by his own appetite – as appears likely at all other times.

Some eagles are not to be trifled with at this stage, and will attack without hesitation; most are much shyer. The female Crowned Eagle of the pair near my house now knows me so well, and has so little fear of me, that she attacks me at once, straight out of the nest, when she has small young. I am very much afraid of her, and watch her very carefully, for she could do very serious damage. Once she struck me from behind, making deep talon wounds in my flesh.

Most young eagles have to be fed even when partly feathered but the young Crowned Eagle (*Stephanoaëtus coronatus*) can feed itself when almost wholly downy

The growth of the eaglet's tarsus and bill is usually more or less complete once it is feathered. This is probably an adaptation to enable the eaglet to hold and tear up prey unaided. The hind claw, the largest, grows faster than the others, and the eaglet sometimes trips on it when walking about the nest. Some eaglets, notably those of the Crowned Eagle, are precocious, learning to tear up prey while still downy; others depend on their parents for food even when well-feathered. Individual eaglets of the same species vary in their ability to learn to feed, and similar variation occurs between one species and another.

Generally however, once eaglets are feathered all that one sees of the adults is a brief visit when bringing prey. The feathering of the eaglet usually releases the female from guarding and brooding duties, so that she can take part in killing and bringing prey. She usually brings more than the male does for the rest of the fledging period. Whichever parent kills will normally make a good meal itself (as is demonstrated by its crop) before bringing the remains to the nest. The adults are thus more likely than the young to survive in times of scarcity, and there is no evidence of self-sacrificing mother love in any eagle.

A newly-hatched Golden Eagle weighing three-and-a-half ounces (100 grams) will multiply its hatching weight forty times, to about nine pounds (4,000 grams), when it is nearly ready to fly, ten or eleven weeks later. It may actually decrease in weight slightly before it flies, for at the latter end of the fledging period the parents usually bring prey at longer intervals. In some cases even coaxing behaviour, deliberately withholding food apparently to make the eaglet fly, has been recorded, but it is very unusual. Towards the end of the fledging period the young eagle bounds up and down in the nest, flapping its wings. Still later it makes short hops or flights to branches of the nest tree. Males are lighter and more active than females; and where they have been sexed as fledglings are known to leave the nest earlier than females. Young male Crowned Eagles leave the nest five–seven days earlier than females. The sex ratio of young eagles when they leave the nest, in the few cases recorded, is about equal, clearly refuting any substance in the suggestion that in the 'Cain and Abel battle' the larger and fiercer females are more likely to survive.

Young African Hawk-eagle (*Hieraaëtus fasciatus spilogaster*) nearly ready to fly; at this stage they do not fight. The male (right) is the elder but the female (left) will eventually become more powerful

Not every eagle, especially in the tropics, breeds every year, and, since it is unusual for a pair to rear more than one eaglet when they do breed, the reproductive rate is usually less than one per pair per annum. In some cases it is very much less, but the cause is not always what one would expect. In the Crowned Eagle, and probably also in the South American Harpy, the pair breeds only every second year, and has a reproductive rate of about 0.4 young per pair per annum. In the Crowned Eagle this is because the adults feed the young one for up to eleven months after it leaves the nest. With an incubation period of 49 days, a fledging period of about 110 days, and this protracted post-fledging period of 270 to 330 days, the whole breeding cycle takes more than a year, so that the birds could not possibly breed every year. Their reproductive rate of 0.4 young per pair per annum represents eighty per cent of what is possible, after the 'Cain and Abel battle' has eliminated the younger chick.

In temperate climates, Golden Eagles rear from 0.4 to 1.4 young per pair per annum, averaging about 0.8 – or four eaglets in five years – about twice the breeding rate of the tropical Crowned Eagle. The rather scanty evidence suggests that related species of eagles have lower breeding rates in the tropics than in temperate climates. Thus the African Fish Eagle on Lake Victoria rears about 0.6 young per pair per annum, and on Lake Naivasha even less, about 0.5, or one young every two years on average, while the American Bald Eagle (*Haliæetus leucocephalus*) averages 1.2 per pair per annum, in areas not affected by agricultural pesticides.

If all these eaglets survived to adulthood it is clear that in a stable population the adults would not need to live very long to replace themselves. A pair of African Fish Eagles would have reared enough young to replace themselves in four years. However, if only half the eaglets survive to maturity, a pair would need eight years, and if seventy-five per cent of the young died before they were sexually mature, sixteen breeding years per pair would be needed to replace themselves. Since African Fish Eagles are probably not mature till they are at least four years old, we can say that if seventy-five per cent of the young die before they are sexually mature (as appears likely from ringing records of other large raptors such as ospreys or buzzards), the average life of African Fish Eagles in the wild state should be about twenty years (sixteen breeding

Young Crowned Eagle (*Stephanoaëtus coronatus*) wing flapping. The secondaries are almost fully grown, while the primaries are still in the sheath. The wing is enormously broad in proportion to its length

years plus four). However, this estimate is affected by the survival rate of the young.

In the Crowned Eagle, with its habit of rearing one young in every two years (almost unique among birds) the breeding rate is about 0·4 young per pair per annum. In this case, if seventy-five per cent of the young died before sexual maturity, a pair would have to have an average breeding life of twenty years to replace themselves. The evidence is that their breeding life is actually shorter – nine years in one fully recorded female, and averaging about twelve years on the basis of observed changes of mates. Perhaps the advantage of rearing one young every two years, and of the Crowned Eagle's very remarkable and protracted post-fledging period, is that a greater percentage of the young that become independent will survive till adult. If fifty per cent survive, then the adults would only need to have an average life of ten years to replace themselves; this would not be very different from what is observed in the field. In fact, in the Crowned Eagle we may fairly deduce that almost half the young that become independent *must* survive to sexual maturity to maintain a stable adult population.

In some eagles the young are easily recognizable as they are coloured quite differently from the parents. In the Golden Eagle it is possible to gauge the age of young birds by the amount of white in their tail feathers, but in some other species one can do better. In the Bateleur there are several distinct stages of immature plumage, occupying, all told, perhaps seven years before the adult dress is assumed. In Bateleurs about thirty per cent of the whole population is immature – on the basis of a long series of counts all over Africa.

In the African Fish Eagle, a species which is very common, even better estimates can be made. It is quite easy to recognize first-year birds, second-year birds, and sub-adults, the latter varying from birds just developing a dark belly like the adult, to birds in almost full adult plumage; this sub-adult phase may last two years. The average from ten counts at Lake Naivasha gives a population of 113.5 adults and 23.6 immatures of various ages (about seventeen per cent). Among the twenty immatures there were on average about twice as many first-year birds (8.2) as second year birds (5.2) and about 10.2 sub-adults. The figures (which are very much in the preliminary stage of such research) may indicate that about half the immatures reared survive to their second year, but that once they have reached that stage they have a good chance of survival thereafter. If this is so, then an apparently low breeding rate of 0·5 young per pair per annum is probably all that is needed to maintain a stable population of adults, and the African Fish Eagle need not live very long to replace themselves. Unfortunately, in this species the adults are so alike that changes of mate would be difficult to recognize without colour ringing, which is difficult to do.

Young eagles are dependent on their parents for some time after they leave the nest, and it is often stated that when the time comes, the adults will drive them out of the territory – Nature being cruel to be kind. However, such little factual evidence as there is (though it is good and clear for the Crowned Eagle) shows that the parents do not drive their young away, but that when ready, they leave of their own accord and release the adults from their parental duties. Certainly, in Crowned Eagles, the young seem suddenly to realize that they can manage on their own, and disappear. The parents continue to bring food to the nest for a few days, but since the young do not respond, they quickly cease to bring prey and soon start the business of refurbishing the nest for another breeding cycle. Probably this may happen in several other eagles as well; though much more research needs to be done before we can say that it is so. What is evident is that, as in human parents, the lives of adult eagles are to a very large extent determined by the stage of development and behaviour of their young.

Young Bateleur Eagle (*Terathopius ecaudatus*)

CHAPTER SEVEN

Eagles and economics

Fortunately for them, most of the world's eagles are probably still relatively immune from the effects of human economics. Some, however, have been seriously persecuted by man, and one species, the Philippine Monkey-eating Eagle, has been brought to the verge of extinction by man's greed, either for hunting trophies or for the money that can be obtained from specimens for zoos. Fortunately, the more responsible zoos have now agreed not to include this endangered species in their collections; but the outlook for the Monkey-eater is still bleak because of the demand for hunting trophies.

Some of the other eagles have been affected much more by human economics, and have been killed in far greater numbers, but are not yet in danger of extinction through such persecution. If they are endangered, it is as likely to be because agricultural economics now encourages the use of extremely persistent and powerful insecticides. What man is doing to his own environment by continually spraying the countryside with deadly poison has been much debated elsewhere; here we need only consider these effects as they apply to eagles and their survival.

Persecution of eagles, either directly by trapping, poisoning and shooting, or indirectly through poisons designed to kill some other creature, is almost exclusively a feature of civilized countries and civilized man. No primitive peoples have either the will or the means to exterminate eagles wholesale, as has been done in many European countries, North America, and especially in Australia. Indeed, among some African tribes

Bateleur Eagle (*Terathopius eacudatus*) – this species may travel two to three hundred miles per day and will indulge in piracy

OPPOSITE: Golden Eagle (*Aquila chrysaëtos*) with two rabbits, typical live mammalian prey in west Scotland

LEFT: Tawny Eagle (*Aquila rapax*) – beneficial to man as it eats rats
RIGHT: European Sea Eagle (*Haliaëtus albicilla*) – exterminated in Britain because of alleged damage to sheep rearing interests

the old-style tribesmen, lacking modern education, are often such good field naturalists that they know which eagles are likely to be harmful to them and which are not. With modern education, however – which has taken effect during the time I have been in Africa – most of this old-style field knowledge disappears, and sad to relate, anything with a hooked beak and talons is likely to become an object of enmity, whether or not it eats chickens, goats or snakes.

The facts are, and it ought to be clearly understood by now, that most eagles are either neutral or positively beneficial to man. Those, such as Tawny or Long-crested Eagles, that eat rats, are clearly beneficial. Snake eagles that eat snakes (rightly or wrongly feared or hated by primitive and civilized man alike) are regarded as beneficial, but are probably neutral or even slightly harmful. Sea and fish eagles eat fish that man could eat, but often in a dead or dying state, such as the Pacific salmon, or species such as catfish or lungfish, that are themselves damaging to fishery interests. The forest eagles such as Harpies, Crested Eagles, or Crowned Eagles, can be called neutrals as they live on animals that scarcely affect man one way or another. All but half a dozen species are, in fact, either clearly neutral, or beneficial to man.

A specialized interest is in game preserving, and where this is important eagles become enemies to man where they would not otherwise be so regarded. Gamebirds are very often crop pests, so that primitive people tend to regard eagles that eat gamebirds with indifference, if they think about it at all. In Scotland, however, and in Europe (but not seriously in America or Australia) the game preserver has been a more bitter enemy of eagles than the shepherd or fisherman; and the fact that eagles have survived in the face of long continued and often quite determined persecution by gamekeepers is good evidence of their ability to survive in adverse circumstances.

The half dozen or so species of eagles that might be considered possibly injurious to man are all large and powerful birds. They include the European Sea Eagle (*Haliætus albicilla*), which was exterminated in Britain – probably unjustly – in the nineteenth and early twentieth century because of alleged damage to sheep-rearing interests. No other species of sea eagle is systematically persecuted, for the American Bald Eagle (otherwise a likely victim) is the United States' National Emblem – which does not always save it from being shot. The remainder are the Golden Eagle, Verreaux's Eagle, the Wedge-tailed Eagle, and the Martial Eagle, all persecuted to a greater or lesser degree because of the damage they do to sheep-rearing interests. Other quite 'innocent' species such as the Spanish Imperial Eagle (*Aquila heliaca adalberti*), now reduced to perhaps a hundred birds, may have suffered from the same cause.

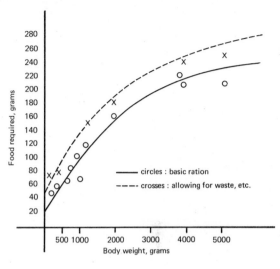

Daily food requirement, diurnal raptors, related to weight

Pole trap with Kestrel (*Falco tinnunculus*) caught by the leg

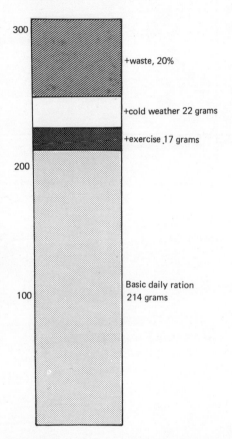

Total daily kill, 316 grams

300

+waste, 20%

+cold weather 22 grams

+exercise 17 grams

200

Basic daily ration
214 grams

100

Daily Food Requirement Adult Male Golden Eagle
Weight 3,700 grams

Enormous numbers of some of these large eagles have been killed, especially of the Golden Eagle and the Wedge-tailed Eagle. Although more publicity has been given to the American extermination of the Golden Eagle in Texas and other southwestern states, probably far more Wedge-tailed Eagles have been killed in Australia. Tens of thousands were killed annually for many years in West Australia and Queensland; yet Australia is so large and thinly populated that the species, though reduced, holds its own. The story in the United States is sadder. An Audubon Society report by Walter Spofford estimates that at least 20,000 eagles were killed by shooting from aeroplanes on the southwestern states in twenty years. Many of these were migrants from further north; but the small local resident population was exterminated in the process.

One is bound to ask whether this killing was ever necessary; whether it was sanctioned on sound grounds, or whether it was based on guesswork and prejudice. The answer seems to be that it was invariably the latter. In no case has the behaviour of the eagle been properly investigated *before* large numbers have been killed. Large numbers are killed and then, because conservation interests raise an objection, the matter may or may not be properly investigated. Where it has been investigated the invariable result to date is that the damage, if any, was grossly exaggerated, and that the killing was unnecessary.

I know of no published results in the case of the Australian Wedge-tailed Eagle, though I believe a detailed survey of that species' habits is in progress. It is, however, well enough known on general grounds that the Wedge-tail feeds mainly on rabbits, and that if it takes lambs, they are probably already dead; one can find this statement in books half a century old, and it should have penetrated by now. There are certainly no known good grounds for persecuting the Wedge-tailed Eagle, and several good reasons for not doing so.

In the case of the Golden Eagle in the southwestern United States, the area affected is one in which a wintering migrant population concentrates, and where sheep and goat ranching has become more important in recent years, partly because the depleted range can no longer maintain cattle. Sheep and goats have increased from a few thousands to over ten million over the last thirty to forty years. The eagles are said to have done so much damage that wholesale shooting from aero-

planes was justified. The suggestion is absurd and can be refuted by a little simple arithmetic.

The Audubon report referred to stated that the *total* estimated population of eagles in North America, on the basis of known territorial requirements of twenty to sixty square miles per breeding pair, might be between 8,000 and 10,000, producing annually about 2,500 young. Not all of these winter in Texas, though about half may do so. Even if they did, and even if they ate nothing but lambs from October to March, they could not have a serious effect on the total number of lambs and kids produced. A Golden Eagle has a daily requirement of about eight-and-a-half ounces (240 grams) of food. It will eat twice that amount when hungry, then go without anything for a few days, like other eagles. Several will feed on one kill, or an individual will feed more than once on the same kill. Supposing that almost the whole eagle population (10,000) of North America concentrated in this area for the entire winter, and ate nothing but lamb or kid, their total

Red Grouse (*Lagopus lagopus scoticus*) – a bird which effectively ensures the killing of eagles in many parts of Scotland to this day

food needs would be equivalent to about 600 lambs or kids per day, that is 18,000 per month or 108,000 per year. The more probable wintering population of 5,000 to 6,000 would need only half this amount. The total population of sheep and goats would need only half this amount (54,000). The total population of sheep and goats in the area approximates ten million; and even allowing for low birth rates in such arid country, they should produce about six million lambs and kids.

Thus, the maximum possible kill of the probable winter population of Golden Eagles in the southwest United States is demonstrably less than one per cent of the lambs and kids born, and the eagles could not conceivably have had any serious effect on the sheep and goat-rearing industry. Moreover, they do not eat live lamb and kid alone, but feed largely on jackrabbits and carrion. In such arid country, lamb losses are certain to be high anyhow, so that one can see how absurd the whole contention is. The fact that the only way in which this slaughter could be curbed was by saying that Golden Eagles might be mistaken for the Bald Eagles which are the National Emblem, is a fair comment upon the ability of law-makers in the United States to act on a sensible and straight-forward basis.

Probably very much the same sort of thing applies in the case of the Australian Wedge-tailed Eagle. In Scotland, the Golden Eagle can, by a similar arithmetical process (better supported by direct observation) be shown to have a negligible effect upon sheep stocks or even, where the latter are healthy and numerous, as in the eastern highlands, on grouse populations. In Sutherland in 1967, for instance, I calculated that in every eagle's territory there would be 600–700 dead lambs available for picking up. The eagles could have fed their young entirely on lamb during the fledging period without having to kill. The evidence was that they took few lambs, and lived mainly on grouse and ptarmigan.

In this area eagles are not considered real enemies by the shepherds and they are in no danger from this source. Most Scottish shepherds and gamekeepers are hard put to recall when they have actually seen an eagle kill a lamb, though all who have studied the Golden Eagle have found remains in eyries. J. D. Lockie, who investigated this question thoroughly, found that eagles did kill a few lambs; it would be, as Seton Gordon remarks, very surprising indeed if they did not.

Golden Eagle (*Aquila chrysaëtos*) with stoat, another mammal that is regularly taken live as prey

However, the number of lambs killed per pair per annum might only be one or two, certainly less than five; and who could say that these lambs were not sickly and might not have died anyhow?

In South Africa Verreaux's and the Martial Eagle have been persecuted because they are said to kill many lambs. Here we are dealing with resident species, inhabiting definite home ranges which, in Verreaux's Eagles, are estimated at twenty-five square miles of semi-arid Karroo country. The population of rock hyrax in such an area is estimated to be the equivalent of 6,000 to 25,000 lbs (2,720 to 11,330 kg.) per square mile, or 150,000 to 410,000 lbs. (68,000 to 185, 250 kg.) per home range. When there is such a superabundance of hyrax available in relation to a total annual food requirement of about 450 to 500 lbs. (200 to 220 kg.) per pair, it is most unlikely that Verreaux's Eagles would take large numbers of lambs. Indeed, the eagles would be totally incapable of exerting any very marked control on the hyrax population which, through the thoughtless killing off of predators, has risen to a level where it is a serious competitor for food with sheep, and does more damage to sheep-rearing interests than the predators themselves. The Martial Eagle is even rarer than Verreaux's, with a larger home range in the wild state, so it is even less likely to have any serious effect on sheep, though perhaps individual Martial Eagles may take more lambs than individual Verreaux's Eagles.

Objective, unbiased assessment of the real effects of eagles on economic matters concerning man's domestic stock thus shows that even those few species that are regarded as harmful are in practice so relatively harmless that they can be safely ignored. There is, in fact, no good reason for active persecution of any species of eagle on the grounds of real economic damage to man's interests. They can safely be let alone to delight those who enjoy watching them, though odd individuals that may actually prefer a diet of lamb or chicken, may have to be eliminated.

However, in civilized countries, it is questionable that eagles will survive – if not because of direct persecution, then for other reasons. There is, alas, good evidence to show that in some areas, notably in Florida with the American Bald Eagle, and in Scotland with the Golden Eagle, that the use of modern potent insecticides has reduced the breeding success of eagles, as it has of other species of carnivorous and fish-eating birds, such as the Peregrine Falcon, European Sparrowhawk, and such birds as Pelicans. In Wester Ross, Scotland, breeding, estimated at over seventy per cent before 1961, dropped to about thirty per cent between 1961 and 1964. It was thought that this was due to the widespread use of Dieldrin in sheep dips, the eagle ingesting this chemical when feeding on carrion in winter.

Breeding success in Scottish Golden Eagles is now the subject of a detailed study by the Royal Society for the Protection of Birds. It is too early yet to say what the eventual result may be. But we have seen that Scottish Golden Eagles normally reared about four young in five years before Dieldrin was in common use. If such a reproductive rate was vital for the maintenance of stable populations of adult Golden Eagles, halving it could result eventually in a catastrophic decline of adult eagles. However, one cannot say whether this will be so. Fewer adults holding home ranges could result in lower winter death rates among the young, and a greater number of young reared to maturity. I at least take some heart from the fact that in many areas of Scotland the population of adult Golden Eagles has not seriously declined in the last decade, and they will probably be there for many a year. And anyone who wishes to add to our knowledge of as yet unstudied species of eagles, such as the species inhabiting South American forests, will probably be able to find undisturbed pairs living perfectly natural lives for as far ahead as we can now see.